To Alan and Muriel,
Who will, we are sure, forgive
our obvious pride in our
talented relation,

   With love

David and Kay.   Jan 1995.

_____

CONTENTS

INTRODUCTION

For three decades I travelled the world, making gardens – and leaving them. I was the most frustrated of gardeners until my husband Brian and I stopped the clock ticking on our nomads' life and settled in the Far North of New Zealand in 1986. Seven years later, six of which comprised brutal gorse-to-garden labour, I have made the last, the best and most beloved of my gardens.

I began writing this book on long winter evenings, when the demon garden allows one to sit by the fire, to luxuriate in armchair gardening with glossy catalogues, to read (gardening books), to sew and to think. I have tried to collect together the loose strands of memories, to embroider between these pages, not with sewing silks but with words, the multi-coloured tapestry with which my garden-making has filled and enriched my life.

The potpourri of stories which have emerged are of the garden and gardening, but they do not command you to set book aside and rush to boot and spade, nor do they explode with terrifying remarks like 'Now is the time to thin out the leeks', or 'Thou shall (or shall not) . . .'. Rather, they invite you to fasten the seatbelt on your armchair; to fly with me to gardens of the past and present; to read of another gardener's trials and toil; to linger; to watch the seasons turning; to garden, and to laugh.

CHAPTER ONE

THE FIRST GARDEN

I think a first garden must be like a first love — one never forgets either.

Once upon a time, more years ago than I care to remember, I went to London to be a student. My minuscule flat was in the basement of a tall terraced house, where only a half of my one window was above ground level. My view was into a tiny square measuring about three by three metres. It was sunk well below pavement level, gloomy and hemmed in by handsome Victorian wrought-iron railings. The square was filled to the base of the railings with a spectacular jumble of old beer and milk bottles, clothes, shoes, cans, newspapers, bicycle bits, the wrappings of many a good fish-and-chip supper from the chippie up the road, cigarette butts and packets — and the corpse of an old tailor's dummy, which I did not like to see when I came home late at night.

Each week I cleared a layer of the debris of street life into my small dustbin. This improved the level of the view through my half-window mightily. When I finally reached the awful depths of the last layer, what looked unbelievably like patches of soil began to appear. It was indeed soil, albeit compacted to rock hardness by years without cultivation and probably by the weight of the rubbish on top of it. Sour, sooty soil, lacking in any plant nutrient whatsoever – unless one counted the endless rotting fish skeletons from the fish-and-chip suppers.

I was ecstatic. I had a square of earth – a garden! And so began the Garden of Ignorance.

I rushed out to buy a gardening tool from the junk shop on the corner and came back well pleased with a large trowel, a bargain because the handle was a bit loose. (No room in my tiny student pad for the gardening accoutrements of the experts, such as spades or hoes.)

It did not occur to me that I should dig over, fertilise or prepare my precious plot in any way. I walked to and from college (a long way), saving my bus fares so that I could spend the money on plants. I haunted the street stalls and barrow boys and came away deliriously happy with pots of the brightest and the best – stiff hot-house carnations with no scent, rigid tulips of awful scarlet and yellow, tender 'wilt-at-a-look' pots of gypsophila, Corporation flowerbed salvias of screaming red, and squat orange marigolds. All were mine . . .

The *pièce de résistance*, of which I was inordinately proud, although it made things a bit cramped, was a Hybrid Tea rose with fat cabbage-shaped blooms of puce.

The gardening began in earnest. Out came the bargain trowel, and I chiselled holes in the unloving and polluted soil for my treasures. In they went. With an old saucepan, I watered them well, because I knew one should do that. I didn't worry too much when the water skidded straight off the impervious face of my beds. If there had been a Society for the Prevention of Cruelty to Plants, I would have been found guilty of many offences punishable by hanging.

How those poor plants struggled to grow in my inhospitable, murky square. They became anaemic of complexion. They grew long and lanky, raising their heads desperately to the patches of sunlight and sky, which were almost shut out by tall buildings. Their foliage became thick with the clouds of dust flung up by the buses and never-ending traffic. I doted on them, but they did not flower, and I was sad.

My milkman was a sore trial to me. He would eye my leggy treasures with a cheeky East End grin and say, 'Wot, you tryin' ter start a gardin, or sumfink? You wanner come up my allotment an' see 'ow fings grows there – plenny-er-good manure, thas wot you need in there.'

'Plenny-er-good manure' was about as inacessible to me in my student lifestyle as a degree diploma was to him in his. And it was to be several decades before there were writers like Beth Chatto to teach one about planting in difficult areas, and before the printing of gardening oracles with titles such as 'What to Plant in Concrete Soil in Dark London Basement Gardens'.

The neighbourhood cats took over my garden and made merry with nocturnal feline orgies – bringing more instant plant death. I took to treating myself to rides on the bus again and to saving shoe leather.

It was at this stage that a visiting aunt with home and garden in lush and lovely countryside, contemplating my Garden of Ignorance with a wry smile, said, 'I will send you some iris rhizomes.' The parcel duly arrived, out came the trowel again, and with a distinct lack of enthusiasm, I hacked holes for the dull-looking 'roots'. I watched their planting spaces for a while, but nothing happened and I forgot about them.

One April morning, when all the London parks and squares were awash with colour and the froth of cherry blossom, through the layers of rubbish, which had started to reclaim my garden again, sword-like new leaves rose up, tall and wonderfully green. I watched them daily, and when fat buds formed on tall stalks, I would fuss about among them, pointing out their miraculous appearance to any passer-by who would listen to me.

Quite suddenly my inhospitable garden became a sea of magnificent flag irises, making a great splash of purest Monet blue in the grey city street. People would point down at my flowers from the top of buses, and passers-by would stop and gaze at them with pleasure. (I think it was at this precise stage in my life that I became infected by the terminal disease called gardening which afflicts so many of us.)

Today, I have a daughter who is herself a student in London. When I visit her, it is my turn to look down into basement gardens from the top deck of the red buses. They are paved now with smart tiles, and filled with beautiful pots and containers, spilling over with colourful – and healthy – plants.

I no longer remember the name or variety of the rhizomes, but now, many years and many gardens later, when my spade has almost turned full circle and my gardens at Valley Homestead are looking quite mature, I cannot recall any flowers which surpassed the pleasure so pure given me by those lovely blue irises. I have planted many of the species here, in this (hopefully!) last garden, and each year when I study their loveliness, wishing I could freeze them in a moment of time, each and every one brings back memories of my poor square and of how youthful enthusiasm, hand in hand with blackest ignorance, in the end made a garden there.

She knew. She knew flowers not only by their names – English and Latin – not only by their families, nor their structures, nor their habits – she knew them in their essence.

It is extraordinarily difficult to exlain what I mean, but if you had seen her bend over a winter iris, you would realise what I meant. . . . There was magic in her touch. At any rate, the iris over which she had bent was the only iris which bloomed that winter.

Beverley Nichols
Down the Garden Path (1932)

CHAPTER TWO

THE THWARTED
GARDENER

Three decades were to elapse between the making of my Garden of Ignorance and the gardens at Valley Homestead, and through all those years I was to remain a thwarted gardener. Having left university, I went to Malaysia to teach and there met the proverbial dashing young army officer who was to make me an army wife. We moved every two years, and I made gardens all over the world – and left them.

In each of my husband Brian's postings we would move into an army house called a 'quarter'. The size varied according to rank and seniority, but they all had interior decor, carpets, curtains and furniture that were horribly identical.

Shortly after moving in, the packing crates would arrive. I would organise my instant household, whizzing the furniture around to new positions just for the hell of it. No matter where we were in the world, as soon as our personal ornaments, pictures, books and toys had given the quarter some semblance of individuality, out and away I would go to suss out the latest conditions for garden-making. The foreknowledge that I would have to leave whatever plant paradise I created in a brief two years never seemed to deter me – I guess I just never learned!

In the more remote postings there were sometimes not

enough official military quarters. Then the army would rent private houses locally for its families, called 'hirings'. The loveliest of our hired homes were vast, rambling planters' bungalows on tea or rubber estates in Malaysia. Here I had unlimited acres and I made exotic, flamboyant (and probably very vulgar) tropical gardens.

One did not make flowerbeds as such. These provided homes and snug nesties for undesirable garden residents such as snakes, scorpions and vast, hairy spiders. They also created hiding places for armies of giant ants whose jaws could be heard rasping. I was warned very early by our Malaysian houseboys not to walk barefooted in the garden. It took just a single bite by one of those crocodile-jawed ants to cure me of that habit once and for all.

There were larger pests to contend with, too. Hordes of inquisitive monkeys would descend into the garden in chattering brigand bands. Most of all they liked to eat or steal the washing from the line. (I caused a riot at the swimming club one afternoon by sauntering nonchalantly along the edge of the pool in a swimsuit, which, unbeknown to me, had been eaten into huge holes all around the rear. . .). Next to this diversion, the monkeys' favourite hobby was to pluck and eat the best and brightest of my flowers. Time and again I would come home to a garden of decapitated stalks, with flowerheads chewed or tossed all over the lawns. The husband would blanch visibly, coming home to a wife throwing a grand tantrum at the treetops, to an invisible enemy.

Having contended with garden pests like these during years in the tropics, it is small wonder that in my gardens in other more temperate parts of the world, I would annoy my friends by being disgustingly blasé about the frolics of a few aphids, the frenzies of a few green beetles or the opal trails of slugs and snails.

In gardens of the Far East I used to plant great swathes of oriental lilies, forests of flaming bougainvilleas, huge exotic hibiscus and heat-loving oleanders. I loved planting frangipani trees; like all the other plants in the tropical heat, they grew quickly from cuttings. The memory of the intense fragrance of their waxen white blossoms with golden hearts, after the rain or in the heat of the sun, remains with me still. The Chinese amahs dried the fallen blossoms for making fragrant tea, and the children used to make miniature gardens with them.

Because of those larger species of garden pests, I was never able to make vege gardens of my own, but I used to have great fun helping the camp or plantation gardeners grow wonderful tropical fruits such as pineapples, papayas, lychees, bananas and mangoes.

The tropical garden which caused Brian most anguish was one which I had created on the tiny balcony of a thirteenth-floor flat in a high-rise tower block in Hong Kong. I had a garden planted in some one hundred and eighty pots. At this time I worked quite a distance away and was not always able to get home when typhoon signals were hoisted – which was quite frequently during the steamy Hong Kong summers. Brian would have to rush home from camp and haul all one hundred and eighty pots into the postage-stamp living-room of the flat, so that the winds would not hurl them about.

Not all my gardens were made in sunshine. Whenever we were posted to Europe, we always seemed to arrive in autumn, with long, hard winters ahead, and many were my ice and snow gardens. Over the years I collected a stock of precious bulbs for winter and spring blooming. I had to dig them up each time we moved. As bulbs do, they multiplied with time, and the end of each posting found me agonising over how many I could cram into the corners of packing crates. The family grew used to finding 'half Mum's last garden' in the pockets of their garments or shoes, or in pots and pans. As I made each new garden, the bulbs would be replanted and allowed to put down roots for just as long as I was.

I enjoyed the days of snow when the loved and familiar current garden was lost, blanketed in a silent mantle. There was joy in picking, with snow-numbed fingers, a spray of wintersweet – *Chimonanthus praecox* – golden in flower and almond in smell, or in following a path mapped and stencilled by birdprints.

Winter, with its chameleon face, brought me gardens transformed overnight by sparkling frost, which painted filigree stencils of flowers on windows and paths. The hoar candied the grass with crystal ice, so that each stalk was stiffened and wore seedheads of tiny pearls.

If our army quarter did not have a pocket handkerchief for a garden, there was no admitting defeat. When we lived in great cities, I reverted to windowboxes and hanging baskets. I had pots of tomatoes, courgettes and cucumbers, sometimes a windowbox full of herbs and another of salads. Flowers, or my precious bulbs, would bloom in pots or hanging baskets. There was always a way.

Now our globe-trotting days are over and we have come home to stay, in Northland. The long-suffering husband has awarded me – perhaps in memory of gardens loved and lost – my Long Service and Good Conduct Medals. He has given me a century-old kauri homestead north of Whangarei in a beautiful farm and bush setting.

One-and-a-half acres of virgin paddocks were allotted to garden area, for me to play in and in which to put down roots. It is mine, all mine, not just for two years but for as long as I shall wish. But 'play in'? Well, that's another story!

The trouble with gardening is that it does not remain an avocation, it becomes an obsession.

Phyllis McGinley
The Province of the Heart

CHAPTER THREE

RETURN
TO AOTEAROA

Having ended our nomadic life and made the decision to settle in New Zealand, our requirements, we thought, were simple: a spacious old rural home, with land attached, to house a container-load of large Victorian furniture, the result of two sets of parents' globe-trotting collectomania as well as our own.

In April 1987, many real-estate agents and many houses later, we found the property which fulfilled all criteria. One day, sixteen kilometres north of Whangarei, we drove up a steep track graced with ragwort, thistle, gorse and eroding clay banks. Sitting at the top in a paddock of waist-high grass, looking for all the world as though it had been dropped from the air, stood the century-old rambling villa we were soon to call Valley Homestead.

The house had been built by a wealthy timber merchant for his family in 1898; in later years it served as a large farmhouse. Uplifted from its original site in the Whau Valley area of the city, it had been brought to its present position in 1980. Sadly, the family who had moved it were not able to remain in the house and it was left standing empty for several years. Possums played hide-and-seek in the roof, and damp in some parts had caused the scrim to balloon out from the walls in spectacular bulges.

We had been shown so many old homes which, externally, were architectural gems but which had been 'modernised' inside, to make 'shiny vinyls'. We were delighted that the interior of this house had remained intact, even to a pretty old black cooking range in the kitchen. The few structural alterations which the home required could be done by us and kept in harmony with its era and character.

We were further fortunate in that the previous owners had completed the major renovation work of rewiring, replumbing and reblocking, so that the old home, though still in need of some restoration, was structurally sound. We were grateful, and felt good-humoured about other tenants' predilections for walls of smoked-mirror tiles and navy-blue tartan, and for topping off a hundred years of paint layers with fluorescent kingfisher-blue.

The siting of the house is superb, and we bless the family who moved it here for their vision. We have an uninterrupted rural view from every window, and the home sits in perfect privacy and peace, in the centre of its nineteen hectares of farmland. It has a backdrop of a small mountain of native bush and looks down on wide, flat plains of pastureland which was once a vast kauri forest. The land became very swampy and, despite the spending of millions of dollars to drain it, it is still referred to as 'the Hikurangi swamp'. The name of the small settlement around the house is Kaurihohore, 'place of the kauris'.

Naming our new home came easily. We had kept a home base in England during our nomadic years as a military family – a much-loved, rambling old house in a small village in Hampshire, an anchor and an oasis through years of travel. It had been named 'Long Valley' for the low tract of land it overlooked. It seemed a natural progression to name our old Northland villa 'Valley Homestead'.

The programme of restoring the interior of the house with decor suitable to its era took place during our first year of residence, while Brian established our business in Whangarei. As I tried every method of stripping paint known to man (there is only one way – the hard way), hung wallpaper and produced curtains hot from the sewing machine, I would gaze dreamily out across the rough paddocks, planning the garden. In retrospect, I realise how valuable this period of incarceration was, because it prevented me from rushing out and merrily making beds here, there and everywhere. Lengthy observation showed me which areas were the most sunny and dry, which were damp or shaded, and which were most open to the wind (always to be my enemy), and I planned the garden layout accordingly. I had no idea at that time just how terminal a 'disease' making this garden would become.

Towards the end of the house-refurbishing year, Brian was able to take time out from the business, and we set up a husband-and-wife demolition team pretty smartly. We needed to clear large areas of paddock around the house for the foundation layout of the gardens. Our worst problem was that the whole area over which the front looked was solid concrete. This had been the foundation layer for a large barn-cum-house, which had been demolished to make way for the arrival of Valley Homestead – sawn in half right down the middle.

We had neither the equipment nor the expertise for breaking up the concrete ouselves, so we contracted two hefty Kiwi friends to help. Though it was such a large area, they thought the job would be straightforward enough until, wielding sledge-hammers like toothpicks, they found the concrete to be heavily reinforced with metal rods and bars. Several days of brutal toil made it obvious that it was a job for pneumatic drills. *Finis*, my grand plans for large flat pieces of concrete for garden walls, paths and other landscaping . . .

Even under drills and pounding sledge-hammers, that concrete had a will of its own. Each evening when he came home,

Brian paled to see how small an area had been broken up. He grew paler by the day as costs mounted, and in the end we had to pay to have the great heaps of shattered rubble and twisted metal bars taken away. This expense didn't do too much for our initial garden-making budget.

While our burly friends had been wreaking havoc on the concrete, as a little light entertainment from shovelling up mountains of rubble, we had been demolishing ramshackle fences and farm buildings from areas allotted to become garden, and chainsawing to the ground a truly horrible twelve-metre-high bamboo hedge. It served no purpose, not even that of a windbreak, thrust out lusty canes to impede passage of man and vehicle along the drive, and shut out the view of our bush-clad mountain. Our neighbours, who were immensely kind but secretly amused by the antics of the new 'Pommie cockies' on the hill, with great Kiwi good humour put up with conflagrations of bamboo which burned for a month.

CHAPTER FOUR

THE GREAT DIG

When we had reduced the waist-high paddocks around the house to resemble something like a lawn, the homestead stood stark and naked. It looked as though at the blink of an eye, or a sweep of wind, it would uplift itself and take off again. I knew I had to root it to the ground on which it now stood. This would only be achieved by digging and planting beds under the verandas on all four sides of the house. So began the era of 'Diana's Great Dig'.

Every day I cut squares of paddock turf thick with kikuyu, paspalum, carrot weed and any other undesirable pasture grass which is a foe to the farmer. I turned them, split them, broke them and dug, dug, dug. By the end of day one I was possessed of the knowledge that beneath a foot of topsoil lay a solid pan of crude clay, and I had begun a long-term friendship with an interesting soil-breaking tool called a crowbar.

The house covers some three hundred square metres and I dug borders 2.5 metres wide around all sides. Someone somewhere would be able to perform maths to tell me exactly how big an area I dug. I only know that each day began with the spade, blisters and backache, and ended with the spade, more blisters and worse backache!

Dreams of the luscious plants with which I would fill the beds sustained me through the days of brutal toil as blisters turned to callouses. Straightening up to ease my aching back, I would see in my mind's eye misty mauve wisteria racemes cascading from the lacework we had restored on the verandas, and old roses (ever my passion) tumbling in scented, bee-embroidered profusion, all rooting the old house to the land on which it stood.

I have always yearned for wisteria and had tried so hard to grow it around our original home in England. There, in Hampshire, the soil was thin, and full of chalk and flint. It was a classic case of the wrong plant for the wrong place, but gardeners are a stubborn breed. Poor soil, our long absences from home and the winters of the Northern Hemisphere ensured that my poor specimens put all their strength into simply staying alive. After about five years, they produced a few ragged streamers of blooms which were little more than a sad whisper.

When we arrived in Auckland in the spring of 1986, I could scarcely believe the luxuriance of the growth of the wisteria I saw, and I was enchanted by the great cascades of blue and amethyst racemes which misted houses and fences. I promised myself that the first plants which would go into the garden I was to make in New Zealand would be of *Wisteria sinensis*. And so it was; the end of the Great Dig around the verandas of Valley Homestead was celebrated by ceremonial plantings of the lovely climber. Today, six years later, in our kind Northland climate their growth has been such that the birds nest in them and the pruning saw is required to 'trim' them.

There was never any problem for the theme of the garden. The loved gardens of my childhood had been essentially old English, but I did not want to create a total cottage effect devoid of New Zealand's wonderful natives. I wanted to plant the old roses, herbs and perennials for myself and the century-old villa, together with natives for the indigenous birds and other animals, so that the garden in its bush and farm setting would become very much part of the New Zealand landscape.

While I was in the early stages of making the garden, I went on a 'garden safari' organised by a local charity. We visited some twenty gardens; all were beautiful, and a credit to their owners, brim full of old-fashioned roses and perennials, but I had the strangest feeling that I could have been in Kent or Sussex. I felt a little sad about all those 'mini-Sissinghursts' and have always tried since to maintain a careful integration of natives and cottage-garden plants, to form a whole harmonious with our New Zealand environment.

As the days were filled with hard labour, the evenings were filled with mountains of library books on old roses; there were so many to choose from and so many different groups to learn about. Their names were so evocative. I think in those early days I ordered roses such as 'Souvenir de Mme Léonie Viennot', 'Étoile de Hollande', 'Duchesse d'Angoulême' and 'Mme Alfred Carrière' simply because I was seduced by the magic of their names.

I hasten to add that I have never regretted this letting of the heart rule the head. I came to love 'Mme Alfred' madly, so quickly did she reward me with her exquisite scented blooms of white, blushed with the faintest pink; so shyly she dips her head as she romps around the front door. During the winter months I allow *Jasminum polyanthum* to twine through her branches, looking forward to the time it smothers itself in clusters of carmine-tipped, fragrant, star-like flowers. I carry luxurious armfuls of its perfumed beauty indoors to scent the house all winter, and then, one day in spring, 'Mme Alfred' emerges through its glossy foliage, with her blushing white blooms, blending her fragrance with that of the jasmine. They are made for each other.

Fortunately, Kiwi friends had enlightened me about *Jasminum polyanthum*'s wicked rate of growth in the subtropical warmth of Northland. Rather than be denied the plant's winter charms, I placed it in a strong container with a trellis frame, so that the degree of its growth through 'Mme Alfred' could be controlled. Any affectionate tendrils reaching out to embrace everything else in sight can now be sternly snipped off. I also stood the container on a flat paving stone to prevent the wanton one's roots creeping down through the drainage holes into the soil.

For fun, as all the newly dug beds were beneath the windows of the house, I planted roses to match the decor of the rooms within. Honey-scented 'Buff Beauty' drapes herself gently around the dining room, her nodding, frilly heads of apricot-yellow matching the golden tones inside. Velvety vermilion 'Étoile de Hollande' echoes the cream and crimson of the master bedroom and the soft pink goblets of dainty 'Duchesse d'Angoulême' complement the apple-green and rose printed chintz of the kitchen areas. Tall-growing 'Queen Elizabeth' peeps through the sitting-room windows, intermingled with the old parchment blooms of 'Diamond Jubilee', melting into the tranquil buffs and pink inside. Though the beauty of the shape and form of many roses compensate for their lack of perfume, those planted for my 'window dressing' schemes were chosen very much for the fragrance with which they surround the house.

Other roses planted in this joyous first selection of those early days included the Rugosa 'Blanc Double de Coubert', the old 'muslin rose' which has petals like white tissue paper folded with stamens of gold and with an exquisite fragrance. Companion to 'Blanc Double' is 'Rosa Mundi', a rose of ancient lineage. Her satin blooms of creamy white splashed with vermilion are often portrayed on mediaeval European tapestries and samplers. The velvet vermilion of the petals, and the stamens of quivering gold of old roses such as 'The Herbalist', 'Tuscany Superb', 'Alain Blanchard' and 'Cardinal de Richelieu' always remind me of the rich embroidery worked on the velvets and damasks worn by Elizabethan princes and princesses, sumptuous fabrics with which the roses share their names.

Favourite of the roses with softer tones, the incomparable Wichuraiana 'Albertine', all fragrant coppery salmon, romps around the lacework on one side of the house, and 'Cecile Brunner' tumbles with miniature blush-pink flowers of exquisite Hybrid Tea formation, no larger than a thimble, from the other.

Not all the roses with which I filled the beds were old in the truest sense. I have always enjoyed the David Austin English roses, which combine the scent, form and colour of the old roses with the repeat blooming of modern cultivars, and with which they mingle perfectly. 'Graham Thomas', with abundant blooms of lemon-gold, 'Abraham Darby', a soft, coppery pink, 'Heritage', cupped prettily in fragrant blush-pink, and 'Mary Rose', which resembles the loosely petalled clear-pink damask roses, have become special favourites.

Much loved, too, is gay little 'Mutabilis'. Pointed flame-coloured buds open to lemon single flowers, which change to deep pink and coppery crimson, and are borne with such abundance that the whole bush looks as though it is covered with butterflies. 'Jean Ducher', with cupped flowers of soft peach shaded with pink, has exquisite fragrance, and I have to harden my heart to prune her when she looks set to bloom all winter.

The last of the beds of 'The Great Dig' was the one under the south-facing side of the house. Because this bed is lightly shaded, I intermixed old roses with fuchsias, which I think is always a pleasing combination; the roses did not seem to mind the semi-shade. The colour theme is mainly of lavender, pinks and soft mauvey purples. 'Lavender Dream', with prolific flowers of soft mauve-pink, multi-petalled lilac 'Anaïs Ségales', and the shell-pink English rose 'Heritage' are underplanted with the cream and lavender ballerina flowers of *Fuchsia* 'Boudoir' and the muted light lilac and carmine flowers of *F.* 'Aunt Juliana'. This fuchsia also complements the singing carmine-pink petals of the climbing rose 'Parade', which gives just the right amount of zest to the lavender tones. In winter, underplantings of violets, lavender polyanthus and *Primula malacoides* give colour when little sunlight reaches the area.

I thought the day would never come, but at last 'The Great Dig' really was over. Three sides of the house were folded into beds of massed roses underplanted with old-fashioned cottage-garden plants such as delphiniums, foxgloves, lavenders, penstemons, violas and nicotianas. Bordering the beds, *Rosa* 'The Fairy' spills her small pink blooms over companion plantings of catmint, pinks and lambs ears, *Stachys lanata*.

Despite all this talk of romance and roses, my days at this stage were still those of an Irish navvy and were to remain so for several more years. The silk frocks and pearl necklaces of the army officer's wife now belonged to another life. Once delicate, lady-like hands sported impressive callouses, were ingrained with soil and lacking in fingernails, but I was bronzed, fit, could swing a crowbar or pickaxe with the best of them and was blissfully happy!

'Established' is a good word, much used in garden books,
'The plant, when established' . . .
Oh, become established quickly, quickly, garden
For I am fugitive, I am very fugitive. . . .

Those that come after me will gather these roses,
And watch as I do now, the white wisteria
Burst in the sunshine, from its pale green sheath.

Planned. Planted. Established. Then neglected,
Till at last the loiterer by the gate will wonder
At the old, old cottage, the old wooden cottage,
And say, 'One might build here, the view is glorious;
This must have been a pretty garden once.'

Ursula Mary Bethell (1874-1945),
'From a Garden in the Antipodes'

CHAPTER FIVE

THE BRIDES' WALK

A truckload of topsoil was brought in to transform the concrete dust in front of the house to the velvet lawn I saw in my mind's eye. Before spreading the soil and sowing, we excavated a small ornamental pool. It was a basic procedure. We measured the required shape, of classical design, dug the hole and lined it with a layer of sand to prevent sharp stones piercing the double layer of heavy-duty polythene used as the pool liner. We used old red bricks to seal the edges, to match the three-tier layer of steps we had built nearby, leading down from the verandas. I then set to, with barrow and shovel, spreading the mountain of topsoil, laying the whole of the rest of the area in front of the house in lawn.

Weather conditions were favourable, and tiny green blades appeared quickly. I was just anticipating the first mow when Daisy, our nursing cow, got out (as only nursing cows can) with her two calves. During her extensive walkabout she sank her huge hoofs some fifteen centimetres deep all over the new lawn, making cavities which filled with water during showers. Her calves had executed a Wild West rodeo stampede and were apprehended, all long-lashed innocence, with mouthfuls of perennials from the new rosebeds. The little new grass they hadn't eaten they had crushed underfoot.

I suffered an attack of red spots before the eyes, spent a

26

dipsomaniac evening, and went out next day to lay the lawn all over again. There seemed to be a jinx on that lawn; from the day I relayed it, we went into severe drought. I managed to nurse the germinating seeds by recycling enough household water to supplement our limited rural supply, and they somehow survived.

As the drought grew more severe, the brickwork Brian had laid so carefully around the pool began to look distinctly lopsided. He had spent hours crawling around with the spirit level, and his work had been perfect. We realised that the clay pan (on which the whole garden sits) was contracting into cracks beneath the soft topsoil of the new lawn, causing subsidence – just enough to tilt the bricks slightly. By the time the drought had ended they had settled down, and we had grown used to their slightly tumbled appearance. We told ourselves that the brickwork 'looked as though it had been there for a long time' and 'had character', rather than uplifting it and laying the lawn for a third time.

With autumn and the return of the rain, it was time to make the next area of garden, this time in the narrow area, some twenty metres long, bordering the east side of the house. As it was only seven metres wide, the corridor-like area suggested a traditional rose walk on my mental landscaping blueprint.

The corridor was hemmed in by a three-metre-high macrocarpa hedge, which was labour intensive, made the area dark and damp, and had to go. Brian chainsawed the trees to bare trunks, leaving them in the ground as the framework for the trellis of old roses with which I planned to border the rose walk. We cut lengths of teatree from the bush to make the crosswise trellis supports. The soil left under the hedge was compacted and poor, and in between working at digging and enriching it for the eventual planting of climbing roses, I planted a formal walk of a double row of standard roses through the middle of the corridor. Each year since, I have had fun experimenting with underplantings of different annuals. This season, fluffy blue *Ageratum* (floss flower) makes a cool blue sea as a foil to the massed colour of the roses.

Autumn finally came, the soil was ready for the roses which were to clothe the trellis, and then I really went to town! In went 'Sombreuil', a creamy white Tea rose with flat, quartered, rosette-shaped blooms sometimes tinted with a blush of peach at the centre. This rose has an exquisite perfume and remains one of my great favourites. Empress Josephine's Bourbon 'Souvenir de la Malmaison' is 'Sombreuil's companion, gorgeous with blush-pink, globular flowers, and 'Mme Alfred Carrière' completes the pastel trio.

Moving to deeper tones, the Tea rose 'Lady Hillingdon' displays long, elegant buds opening to large, loosely formed blooms of apricot-gold. 'Gloire de Dijon', a Noisette from my childhood and cottage gardens of yesteryear (when it was called 'Old Glory') spills buff-yellow, perfumed blooms next to the lovely 'Meg', whose beauty on the trellis opposite my studio window often causes my fingers to still over the keyboard of the word processor. She has huge, almost single flowers of clear pink, with rich apricot at her heart and a mass of maroon-gold stamens. I feel quite passionate about her.

Pretty little 'Cornelia' is the companion of 'Meg', offering many-flowered trusses of small frilly blooms of coppery apricot which are sweetly Tea-rose scented and bloom with profusion over many months. 'Cornelia' leans into the singing pink of the Bourbon 'Zéphirine Drouhin', who smothers herself with cascades of deep rose flowers for the whole summer. She plays neighbour to the free-flowering 'Gerbe' rose, a Wichuraiana which has small clusters of soft pink tinted with cream, and a delicious peony-like fragrance. Next door, the dainty, feminine, double blooms of clear pink 'Clair Matin' reach across the trellis towards 'Tausendschön', the 'Thousand Beauties' rose. She lives up to her name, trailing long branches laden with clusters of small blooms in many shades of pink – a gay and lovely rose.

The pink roses merge into golds and yellows with the butterfly single lemon flowers of 'Golden Wings', which are not unlike those of the unruly 'Mermaid'. When the petals fall, a heart remains of stunning mahogany-brown stamens, which look like burnished gold when the sun catches them. Equally lovely, and another favourite, is the Musk 'Buff Beauty', which gives honey-apricot blooms and shiny rich green foliage.

David Austin's English rose 'Graham Thomas', with Tea-rose fragrance, is a star with large, massed blooms of golden yellow. The trellis ends with the fernlike foliage and single lemon flowers of the cheerful and unusual little rose 'Canary Bird'.

We left a gap in the centre of the trellis large enough for a rustic seat, so that we could sit and look out over the panorama of pastureland below. Brian did not enjoy my rustic-furniture phase. The wood chosen for the artistic endeavour was so hard a hole had to be drilled for the insertion of every nail or screw. Three drill attachments and lots of bloodied fingers later, the seat was complete, strong and intact, and the marriage – shaky. Two large bushes of *Lavandula denticulata* flank the seat, making it a favourite resting-place in the garden. The climbing roses are underplanted with fuchsias and old-fashioned perennials to harmonise with the other beds around the house.

Late in the following spring, when all the new roses were giving their exciting first blooms, a young friend came to visit, to show off her new engagement ring. As we strolled in the garden, she stood at the head of the rose walk and announced, 'That's it. There's my aisle. I'm going to sweep through all those roses on Dad's arm, and get married on the front lawn.' And so she did. This wedding resulted in one of my happiest gardening accidents; before we knew it, another young bride followed in her footsteps, and the rose walk has become The Brides Walk, adding a whole new and joyful dimension to life in the garden at Valley Homestead.

Pruning, planting, propagating,
Hoeing, mowing, digging, sowing,
Forking, fiddling, fertilising.
Weeding, pricking, hosing, picking,
Watching, hoping, nursing, cursing
And long, loving, low-backed labour
For years and years and years.

Pamela Jeffries,
'Making a Garden'

CHAPTER SIX

THE ELIZABETHAN
GARDEN

The Brides' Walk rather forced my hand over the making of the next garden area. Leaving their limousines in front of the garage, the brides wafted along the south side of the house en route to the rose walk. This meant their arrival photographs had a cabbage-patch vege plot set in a paddock of waist-high grass as a background! That wouldn't do at all.

This time it was literally back to the drawing-board, because the geometric squareness of the back of the house and paddock lent itself to the laying out of a garden of formal design. Off to the library, to drown in landscapes designed by Lutyens, Jekyll and William Robinson. Thus inspired, I designed an Elizabethan garden. The basic design was simple, as landscaping of this era often was – roughly a rectangle, bisected by four pathways, converging into a circle in the middle, with a sundial as a centrepiece.

The four quarters of the Elizabethan garden were to be planted to indulge my *grande passion* further, with roses, roses and more roses. But first I had to embark upon my new career as a brickie! Brian was much too busy at this stage, establishing our business in town, to be able to help me, so the bricklaying had to be a fairly basic procedure – no pointing, mortar, spirit levels, etc. for me. I measured the path lines out accurately with twine strung through 'pig tails', and dug them out to a depth of eight centimetres below the soil of the beds. I filled the path lines with builders' sand to make a firm foundation, which also brought them up to the level of the beds.

After all the levelling and groundwork, the exciting moment came of wheeling onto the site my first load of secondhand bricks. When the truck from the demolition yard had dumped them on the drive, it had looked as though there would be enough to build a house. The excitement evaporated pretty fast after I learned that five hundred bricks go virtually nowhere, and how painful to the back and knees path-laying is. I abused my small car for weeks, hauling more bricks from the demo yard, and finally had to restrict myself to laying fifty a day – about a metre in length – for the salvation of back and knees. Suffice it to say, I laid just over two thousand bricks before the paths and circular centrepiece were complete.

A kind friend had given me the cuttings from her hedge of *Lonicera nitida* each time she trimmed it, and I potted hundreds of cuttings over that year with which to plant a low, formal hedge to enclose the garden.

It was a great occasion when I was able to plant the cuttings out. Then came the happy moment of planting the roses, the results of many covetous evenings of study, knee-deep in glossy catalogues. I chose many of David Austin's excellent English roses; 'Abraham Darby' and the delicate pink 'Emmanuel' have become stars in this area.

While labouring over the foundations of the Elizabethan garden, I had been intrigued by an article on Hybrid Tea roses which had held their popularity since the 1940s and were still favourites in 1994. I decided to mix some of these *grandes dames* with other old roses in the Elizabethan garden, to make a colour wheel of dark velvety reds, and pinks, soft yellows and golds, creamy whites, buffs and coppers. The purist would have said, perhaps, that I should have planted a garden of an Elizabethan design with roses of that era, but initial research showed that I should face severe problems with plant availability, so I compromised by including in the companion planting as many old-fashioned perennials and ancient herbs as possible.

In the deep red section of the garden I planted 'Fragrant Cloud' (1964), free-flowering and with unparalleled perfume, 'Josephine Bruce' (1952) and 'Papa Meilland' (1963), both giving blooms of strong fragrance and velvety crimson-scarlet. 'Precious Platinum' (1974) glows dusky red, rivalled by 'Europeana' (1963), which has darkly beautiful trusses of flowers with a fruity fragrance and attractive bronze foliage. 'Rosemary Rose' (1954) has pretty, camellia-like blooms and coppery foliage also. A bed of dark red roses has to be crowned by the incomparable 'Dublin Bay' (1976). Its clusters of large, deep red blooms, borne almost continuously on a strong, hardy plant, will ensure its place on the chart of favourites for many more years to come.

Garden visitors often say, 'I've only got a small garden, but I must have one beautiful rose. Can you recommend just one that is really good?' For this all-singing, all-dancing performer, I would have to recommend 'Dublin Bay' for health, vigour and repeat blooming. If this rose has a fault, it is that its luscious, velvety blooms have little scent. I know that opinions are divided about this, with some gardeners swearing that the rose is heavily scented, and others, like myself, finding little more than an elusive waft. But with so many other virtues, what the heck!

In the pink section I planted 'First Love' (1952), which has long elegant buds of pink with coppery tonings, and 'Nancy Steen' (1976), giving beautiful fragrant flowers of old-fashioned blush-pink with cream and gold hearts. 'Utersen' (1978) smothers herself in frilly, vibrant pink blooms over many months, as does 'Prima Ballerina' (1958), whose flowers are beautifully formed.

The lovely striped cerise-and-white 'Rosa Mundi' also complements this garden.

In the white section I planted the quartet par excellence, 'Pascali' (1963), 'Francis Phoebe' (1979), 'Iceberg' (1958) and 'Margaret Merrill' (1978) – prima donnas all, of delightful shape, form, perfume and performance.

The stunning 'Peace' (1942), begins the section of soft yellows, merging its large blooms with the more delicate rosy salmon petals of 'Dearest' (1960), which have an old-fashioned elegance, and with those of 'Gruss an Aachen' (1909), a grand old lady with large cupped flowers of creamy apricot-pink which are richly fragrant.

The soft yellows give way to the stunning display of creamy buff blooms which 'Diamond Jubilee' (1947) bears, and to the rare parchment and copper tones of 'Julia's Rose' (1976). This unusual rose is a florist's dream, with its subtle colour and long-lasting blooms which have a porcelain translucency. The Floribunda 'Fleur Cowles' (1972) gives scented cream-buff blooms, and the final buff-to-copper rose, which I think is unrivalled for sheer performance, is the excellent 'Nobilo's Chardonnay' (1985). Although not of ancient lineage, this rose's repeat blooming, weather resistance and attractive glossy foliage make it good enough to still be in the catalogues in the year 2000.

Gold tones are added with 'Glenfiddich' (1976) and burnished 'Amber Queen' (1983), the petals of her blooms contrasting beautifully with dark, glossy foliage. The English rose 'Graham Thomas' is also a gold star here, as is the unusual little rose 'Vesper' (1968), which has small, perfectly shaped flowers of buff-apricot. 'Brandy' (1982) and 'Whisky' (1967), sporting richly alcoholic bronze blooms against dark, healthy foliage, complete this brazen section of the Elizabethan garden, favourites all for many more years to come.

At this stage the Elizabethan Garden was not yet complete, but as the newly planted roses gave their first exciting blooms, the brides, straying from the bridal path, found their way in, incorporating it as part of their ceremonial photography venue. They liked to pose, all watered silks, seed pearls, lace and satins, on beaming bridegrooms' arms, ethereal visions in the heart of the garden, among the froth of tiny gypsophila flowers around the sundial's base.

In between weddings I planted the borders of the Elizabethan Garden with *Alchemilla mollis*, much loved in old English gardens. This is a gem of a plant with dainty, roundish, emerald-green, picot-edged leaves, which trap raindrops and hold them like droplets of mercury. In late summer it bears clouds of tiny lime-green flowers like froths of foam.

As the four quarters of the garden bore roses of a different colour, I used herbal plants with silvery foliage, and others with blue flowers, to unify the beds. The tall catmint, *Nepeta faassenii* 'Six Hills Giant', was particularly useful for this purpose, spilling clouds of silvery grey and blues through the lower branches of the roses.

The underplantings of herbs which might have been found in Elizabethan gardens include, in the pink section, tall sweet rocket, *Hesperis matronalis*, whose spires of lavender-violet flowers are intensely fragrant in the evening. *Santolina*, *Pyrethrum* 'Silver Lace', *Artemisia*, *Helichrysum italicum* (the curry plant), and lavenders add to the unifying silver-foliage scheme. The feathery plumes of bronze fennel, *Foeniculum vulgare*, look marvellous with gold roses, but the plants need fairly strict control. Other old-fashioned plants which have found their way into the Elizabethan garden include larkspurs, delphiniums, foxgloves, nicotianas, aquilegias, irises, lilies and cottage pinks.

The sundial within the circular bed at the heart of the garden is underplanted with filmy gypsophila and bordered by blue and gold – dwarf mounds of limey feverfew, *Chrysanthemum parthenium aureum*, and silvery blue catmints. The delightful face of the pansy 'Blue Joker' also makes a pleasing addition.

Bordering the Elizabethan garden on the left was the unattractive side of the garage – a cause for rejoicing, since garden walls are made to be clothed. This was the only one I had, and I was determined to make the most of it. Another lilac-lazuli haze of wisteria (which I still hadn't quite got out of my system) is threaded through with the abundant coppery pink blooms of the old rose 'Souvenir de Mme Léonie Viennot' – perfect companions, and today, five years later, one of the most photographed sights in the garden when they herald spring together.

A final stroke of good fortune in the area was the gap between the end of the garage wall and the rear of the haybarn, a natural alcove which was just perfect for an arbour. Two sheets of trellis for the sides, spanned by three curved roof struts, made a simple and attractive structure. Painted white, furnished with a seat in classical design, here was the arbour to dream in, providing the finishing touch to the Elizabethan Garden areas – roses, bricks, brides and all.

> *Among all the floures of the world the floure of the rose is chief and beeryth ye pryse. . . . For by fayrness they feed the syghte, and playseth the smell by odour, the touch by soft handlynge. And wythstondeth and socouryth by vertue against many sycknesses and evylls.*

> Bartholomeus Angelicus,
> *De Proprietatibus Rerum* (1398)

CHAPTER SEVEN

A TERMINAL
DISEASE

I had revelled, wallowed, luxuriated in my *grande affaire* with all these roses, but the day came, only too soon, when they stood long, leggy, middle-aged and menopausal, desperately in need of an end-of-season *prune*. Clearing the library shelf of 'how-to' books, I studied with diligence, but when I sallied forth, equipped with spanking new secateurs, my menacing thorny thickets bore absolutely no resemblance to the neat little diagrams in the pruning primers.

I joined the Northland Rose Society, a body of cheerful, friendly experts who taught me all there was to know about the dreaded pruning, and about rose care in general. I also learned a good deal about these infatuated rose fanciers, within whose ranks I had become a devout believer. Rosarians have a love of gardening, but, as though this isn't liability enough, they suffer from a further disease which manifests itself in a manic passion for, and obsession with, all things related to the cultivation of the *rose*.

One day we may fall in love with, and plant, just one little mini which flowers profusely and behaves beautifully. Perhaps a bit of the soil in which it is planted gets into our body through the scratches from its thorns, and wham! – we are infected forever. We race to our dangerously near garden centre, where rosebushes just happen to be on 'special' ('Such a bargain, so healthy . . .'). We are hooked. We yield more and more to our new passion. We become avid collectors; we *must* have every new wonder rose that cavorts all over the wretched glossy catalogues the breeders push out each year.

We just know that such dazzling beauties would grow with perfect form, shape, colour and rude good health in our very own beds. Never mind that a second mortgage must be set on the farm, the tyres on the car wear a little balder, the housekeeping embezzled ('The groceries go up in price every week in the supermarket . . .') – they must be ours.

Even Colin Wilson's stern warning in his *Book of Gardens* does not deter us: 'Man was made for better things than pruning his rose trees. The state of mind of the confirmed gardener seems to me as reprehensible as that of the confirmed alcoholic.'

Let no one think that serious rose-growing is a bucolic and meditative occupation. It is an insatiable passion to which the rosarian gives his or her whole heart!

Our conversation gradually becomes peppered with terrifying phrases such as 'budding', 'disbudding', 'grafting', 'deadheading', 'sports', 'suckers', etc., etc. We refer learnedly to '*Rosa* this' and '*Rosa* that', and those of us such as myself who are besotted with the *grandes dames* of yesteryear bandy about names which are totally impossible for the layperson to remember, such as 'Mme Legras de St Germain', *Rosa chinensis* 'Mutabilis' or 'Souvenir de Mme Léonie Viennot'. Such affectation causes the Hybrid-Tea man to roll his eyes heavenwards and make short, succinct comments like, 'Give me a good 'Alexander' or 'Satchmo' any day.'

Old-rose buffs can be further tiresome by pontificating on the vastly complicated family names to which their treasures belong – Spinosissimas, Wichuraianas, Gallicas, Noisettes,

Centifolias – we can go on like this for days.

Rosarians also have an extra manual appendage which ordinary gardeners lack. The extuberance usually sprouts from their right hand in the form of two small curved blades controlled by a spring, which is activated by the depression of thumb and fingers around two short handles.

In addition to censure for being possessed of this extra digit, we have to suffer non-rosarians shaking their heads and muttering 'tsk, tsk' about our image. We are never seen wearing anything but ancient woolly pullies and pants which have been snagged into a thousand tiny thorn tears, so that the strands are unravelled like spaghetti. Any flesh which has been visible is criss-crossed with railway-junction networks of scratches and tears inflicted by our petulant darlings. The prickly ingrates leap out to clutch one and embed thorns into the loving hands which lavish upon them such care.

Rosarians have been known to lose veritable pints of blood during the peak pruning months of July and August, or when they have been weeding among the minis. My daughter, white-faced, lectured me for hours recently when I admitted to mending a wound to a vein with five band-aids. Septicaemia among the rose thorns may sound like a Victorian novelette in which the heroine is in big trouble, but to rosarians such danger is merely an occupational hazard and of little consequence.

Our roses smile when their feet are damp (not wet) and their heads are dry. It follows that we become paranoid about the rain, of which there is always too much or too little. When it is windy (all the time) we are tense and irritable; when both combine to devastate our beauties only days before THE SHOW, we may need counselling, or narcotics.

We are quick to point out to non-rosarians that persons of note through the ages have been stricken with the disease.

Edward Lear, writing to his friend Lord Darlingford in 1885, retaliates with:

> *And this be certain: if be so*
> *You could just now my garden see,*
> *The aspect of my flowers so bright*
> *Would make you shudder with delight,*
>
> *And if you voz to see my roziz*
> *As is a boon to all men's noziz,*
> *You'd fall upon your back and scream —*
> *Oh lawk, oh crikey! It's a dream!*

A.P. Herbert, in his book *Look Back and Laugh*, agonises simply:

> *Greenfly, it's difficult to see*
> *Why God who made the rose, made thee.*

Hereby hangs another tale. *Pests*. Names of insects such as spider mite, sap-sucking beetles and aphids are whispered about with taut lips and furrowed brows. It is over the protection of our darlings from these vampires' fangs that a great divide is caused between rosarians. I hasten to add that we *are* united in that we all have slightly stooped backs from the weight of our backpack spray units, but it is what we choose to put in them which causes rosarian to rise against rosarian.

Some of us drench our blooms with cocktails of toxic chemicals which make 'Agent Orange' seem like a mild detergent in comparison. Others of us go in for witches' cauldrons that boil and bubble stinking organic decoctions of garlic, pyrethrum and even noxious mixes of the green beetles and caterpillars themselves.

Both parties make such exaggerated claims to the efficacy of their pest-annihilation programme that there is nothing for it, at the end of the day, but to agree to differ. Either way, the pests either have extremely bad breath and vacate our bushes for someone else's, or flip over and roll their legs in the air.

The rosarians' 'Great Divide' is also apparent when we are agonising over the health of our pampered ones, who are just a little inclined to sprout dread diseases at the slightest provocation. We twitch at the whisper of mildews, rust and all manner of disfiguring dots and spots. 'Prevention is easier than cure', we hiss, and pour the concoctions into our backpacks.

We discuss our treasures' diet for hours, indulging in impassioned oratory on the virtues (or otherwise) of cowpats, sheep, chook or rabbit droppings. We decree that our roses must be planted in beds of earth enriched by a sacrifice of organisms that conjure up visions of massacre to the non-gardener: bone meal, hoof and horn, dried blood and liquid fish manure.

These machinations merely hint at the extraordinary length to which devoted rose-growers will go in the attempt to produce the perfect blooms which seduced them from the pages of the catalogues in the first place.

I know myself to be incurable, a lost cause to this blighting affliction. The scratched, torn flesh is weak; without my sumptuous, tyrannical, demanding beauties, I should wilt, rust, mildew or break out in a rash of black spot.

There is nothing for it, therefore, but to continue to indulge our passion unbridled, remembering the words of the Reverend Samuel Reynolds Hole in 1869, who positively encourages us in our enslavement by the rose:

> *There should be beds of roses, banks of roses, bowers of roses, hedges of roses, beddings of roses, baskets of roses, vistas and allys of roses.*

The *disease* is deadly.

CHAPTER EIGHT

THE NON-GARDENING HUSBAND

It was the end of another carving-garden-from-crude-clay-wilderness day. The weapons we loaded into the barrow — sledge-hammers, crowbars and pickaxes — to wheel wearily up the drive told their own tale of grinding drudgery. Looking at Brian's tired face and 'I'm-beginning-to-get-fed-up-with-this garden lark' expression made me realise how fortunate I was to have his willing help, knowing how little interest he had in gardening and how much he hated it.

It is not generally realised what a priceless asset the Non-Gardening Husband is. I know I am fortunate enough to have one, and I wouldn't change him for any green-fingered son of the soil. He can (given the right approach) be prevailed upon to push back paddock fences, or ring them with electric wires to defeat bovine appetites — as long as he doesn't have to do anything else. He allows himself to be coerced into giving extra land grants for (another) garden extension, but enthusiastic attempts to involve him in the master plan will send him off quite rapidly 'to check the stock'.

When the mower goes wrong, I do not have to spend days cajoling or nagging Brian to fix it. A computer whizzkid, and pretty clued-up with most things mechanical, he denies all knowledge of the mysterious innards of the mower. Hurling it into the back of the ute, he will drop it into the arms of the mower man in town, and return it, rejuvenated, to me and the lawn a few days later.

We have little water to spare from our rural supply for a large garden. NGH, watching me living out the summer months at the end of the hose, agonising over treasures lost to the drought, took it upon himself to install an impressive DIY irrigation system.

The system involved excavating and building a dam, the digging in by hand of some five hundred metres of alkathene piping, and the provision of 1500-litre storage tank. He may not want to know a trowel from a fork, but the glory of the garden in our scorching Northland summers is more his than mine. To readers enquiring whether he is for hire − 'fraid not.

NGH is happiest and feels most secure in a role of admirer of *the* Garden. Although he scarcely knows the difference between a camellia and a rose, he enjoys what I create, and takes his duties as chief 'Oo-h and Aa-h' fan very seriously. However, despite my best efforts, the extent of his horticultural knowledge does occasionally get us into hot water, proving, when he is caught in the vicinity of the garden by visitors, that a little knowledge is a dangerous thing.

Ingenious though his endeavours are in avoiding this situation, he is sometimes taken by surprise. Collared by a group of guests last summer, he told them that 'those hairy flowers are looking quite good today'. Vanishing then, like a geni, he fled to his study and the embrace of his computer. I was plied with questions from eager gardeners all morning about the hairy flowers. An exotic new perennial? A treasure grown from seed gathered in remote Mongolian steppes?

Later, bearding the lion in his den, I extracted information as to the location of these horticultural wonders. 'Those big things along the drive border' – my best dahlias with the spiky, spidery, cacti petals!

Although incapable, like most Non-Gardening Husbands, of remembering the name of a plant for more than five seconds, he must have a lovely memory of the tree, *Magnolia grandiflora*. He never forgets this one name, and given the chance, likes to amaze visiting townies by just 'mentioning' it. He *will* tell them that our beautiful white Yulan – *Magnolia denudata* – is a *grandiflora*. I do hope not too many visitors have rushed out to buy the latter, and had their homes and gardens smothered in its beautiful but gigantic embrace.

Another hazardous situation for the gardening wife and non-gardening husband team can occur when there is a sudden influx of guests. Recently, two of the three coaches I was expecting rearranged their schedules and arrived simultaneously. With a stiff upper lip, and immense kindness, the husband, seeing me haring around feverishly, offered to host and guide one of them. While they were parking I whipped him around, teaching him the names of the plants which were presently the stars of the garden and about which I knew the visitors would ask.

Exit Samson, with much girding of loins, towards the flood of visitors on the drive, reciting '*Echium plantagineum* . . . "Raubritter" . . . *Cynoglossum nervosum* . . . *Salvia sclarea* . . . "Françoise Juranville" . . .'. Whether he got his Hortus Latinicus mixed up or not I do not know, but he was a big hit. After he had had enough of playing victim and fled 'to the office to look at the GST', I was inundated by fierce old ladies, and starry-eyed young ladies, demanding, 'Where is that nice knowledgeable man? I want to ask him lots more questions, and plant names.' Fortunately, the Yulan magnolia was not in bloom at this time.

The Non-Gardening Husband is the one who, when he can make the time, gives me and the garden the gift of the brutal toil required to build retaining walls, rose poles, sleeper steps and for moving huge rocks. It is he who translates so much of the female gardener's vision into reality, with hard labour; he who abuses his gleaming estate car hauling enormous pieces of driftwood or swamp kauri for landscaping; he who will (cussing) bring the car to a screeching halt when she-who-must-be-obeyed has to leap out in the middle of nowhere to take a cutting from an old rose growing by the roadside. It is he who allows embezzlement of housekeeping funds for sacks of manure and fertiliser, loads of bark or compost, and for the plants among the groceries, which are my weekly fix from the garden centre. He will wade into the pond and drain it for me on a freezing cold day, so that I can remove noxious weeds; he will stand for an hour in the ornamental pool, unblocking the fountain filter.

It is the Non-Gardening Husband who will rush outside with me into the eye of a force-ten gale and shattering rain, to help strengthen the stakes and ties on the roses. It is he who listens with sympathy and with patience to my hair-tearing and breast-beating grand tantrums when the wind has again devastated the garden at its peak; he who will open his wallet when *his* cows have won, and perpetrated a gastronomic orgy on the garden.

Imagine the horror of having a husband like Walter Fish. In her book *We Made a Garden*, Margery Fish says he believed

Firmness in all aspects is a most important quality when gardening, not only in planting but in pruning, dividing and tying up. Plants are like babies, they know when an amateur is handling them. My plants knew, but I didn't. Walter would not tolerate an unhealthy or badly grown plant and if he saw anything which wasn't looking happy he pulled it up. Often I would go out and find a row of sick-looking plants laid out like a lot of dead rats. It became something of a game. If I had an ailing child I was trying to bring round, I'd do my utmost to steer him away from that spot. It didn't often work and I now realise that he was right in his contention that a plant that had begun to grow badly could never be made into a decent citizen and the only thing to do was to scrap it.

Mrs Fish appears to have been dedicated to her Walter. Clearly she had her reasons. I should have considered such hardhearted vandalism as *grounds* if perpetrated by any spouse of mine.

As it is, the Non-Gardening Husband I am fortunate enough to have will never enrage me by demanding, 'What the hell did you dig that bed there for?' or by making scathing remarks like 'Those daft herbs are throwing shade on my tomatoes.' If, like me, you are blessed with one, cherish and nurture him well – his worth is beyond rubies.

CHAPTER NINE

LABRADORICUS
PESTICULATA

During all my garden-making thus far at Valley Homestead, there had always been a canine companion at my side, surveying, supervising, approving – an elderly and much-loved labrador, Bess. So much part of the family, she had come with us from England in 1987, when we settled in New Zealand. Although she was already nine years old, and the cost of her transportation was astronomical, poor Brian had been presented with a 'No Bess, no New Zealand' situation from the female members of the family, and he needed little persuading.

Sadly, several years later, as we completed the Elizabethan garden together, it became apparent that her life was nearing an end. Her frailty led to pneumonia with complications which failed to respond to antibiotics, and the anguishing moment came when I had to stretch out my hand, lift the telephone and ask the vet to come and terminate her life.

It is a paradox I have often pondered, the sad brevity of the lifespan of this most giving, most faithful of man's friends. Bess lies beneath our bedroom window, where the old rose 'Dainty Bess', of mauve-pink, haloed with maroon stamens, blooms above the resting-place of this old and most dear of companions.

With our roots firmly entrenched in the Antipodes, and possession of a small farm in lush and lovely Northland, it was an inevitable progression that not one, but two cream silk labrador puppies of extreme beauty should become residents of home and garden. All large clumsy paws, thrashing tails, and eyes that were limpid pools of brown (sparing them retribution for all sorts of wrongdoing when turned piteously upon us), they were named 'Missy' and 'Amber'. These ladylike names were very shortly replaced by those of 'Killer' and 'Fang', in recognition of their unparalleled sloppiness of nature and total lack of efficiency on the guard-dog front. With admirable self-restraint, I will forego comment upon the havoc they wreaked upon my new gardens in the earlier days of puppyhood.

Dog ownership is fun – ask any gardener. Labradors are an especially rewarding breed. They add a whole new dimension to life in the garden. They have a unique relationship with plants.

Species that are sat/leaned upon by six-stone labradors never recover. Ever. Then there is the 'watering'. It embarrasses me, to say the least, when a visitor, bending down to sniff the fragrance of a flower, has his or her nostrils assaulted by an ammoniac whiff of dog pee. There is also something very peculiar about lady labrador's urine. It will finish forever any pretensions you may have of aspiring to a green velvet lawn. What you will get is an expanse of green liberally blotched with brown, bald patches.

On the whole their lavatorial habits are terrible. Failure to sprint around the lawn with shovel and bucket before a coach-load of guests arrives leaves offended sensibilities – and polluted footwear. Germaine Greer, alias Rose Blight, writing in her *Revolting Garden*, sums up the situation admirably: '. . . plants pecked to death by sparrows, dug up, trodden on, sat on or stolen, or simply annihilated by a blast of animal urine or a cloaking turd . . . '.

Labradors are bad news altogether as far as the turf is concerned. The half tree-trunks which litter the lawns, giving them a very uncouth aspect, are retrievers' sticks. I blanch when visiting gentlemen gardeners hurl these logs the length of the lawn. This is absolutely the best garden sport. A duet executed to perfection by both dogs is the slamming-on of claw brakes at the final moment of retrieval. This results in spectacular skid marks some three metres long. (On the other hand, emergency stops by heavyweight canines do rake up an astonishing amount of moss.)

If a gentleman's aim with the missile is not too accurate, plant treasures raised from seed from expensive catalogues are lost forever. Fragile garden statuary, adorned with cherubs and garlands, topples as the beasts lunge after their tree trunks. Size eight laborador feet are the scourge of the smaller flowers. Their great paws crush them instantly, leaving behind huge splodges some six centimetres deep, which fill with water and add texture to the freshly hoed soil in the rosebeds.

An unexpected bonus from lady-labrador ownership is that the garden inevitably becomes the trysting place to which an endless procession of mangey cattle-dog courtiers beat a passionate and well-trodden path. This causes the rapid demise of a vast number of plant treasures from the 'raised leg' syndrome.

Lady labradors, especially those of youth and beauty, are not renowned for their morals, and the lascivious lovers are welcomed warmly, to say the least. Even with the most elaborate of precautions – bitches under house arrest, etc. – one finds oneself inviting one or both dogs into the car and heading for the vet for a 'morning after' injection with monotonous regularity. The Heinz 57 variety of their suitors, and the inevitable horrendous vet's bills, finally causes one to abandon all ambition of breeding thoroughbred gundogs from ladies whose pedigrees are impeccable but whose morals are disgracefully permissive.

The final decision is made one morning when, dragging smug bitches yet again into the surgery, I hear the young veterinary nurse giggle, 'Here comes Mrs Anthony with her labrawhores again.'

Kind mums, visiting with children, often provide the dogs with balls to play with. They do not know about labradors. Many are the occasions when I have had to break off an impressive garden lecture to placate a screaming child by prising a spitty ball from between slathering fangs.

Bones, burial of – a distressing subject. Rabbits have nothing on labradors when it comes to sniffing out a patch of newly turned earth. This patch instantly becomes number one bone and plant cemetery. Flowers wilt, and shrubs keel over as their root systems are clawed to death and exposed to the elements. Bone interment takes place with frenzied digging, which sends black showers all over the drive or pathways. The merest suspicion that a rabbit might have passed this way results in excavations worthy of the channel tunnel. Raised beds, retaining walls and walkways collapse. The veges look very sick.

Labradors will tell you that the best time for the exhumation of old bones is just before a coachload of guests is due to arrive. This ensures that the nice, newly mown lawn is littered with malodorous skeletal relics. The cool shady verandas, on which the visitors might like to rest, also look good strewn with disgusting rotting bones in advanced stages of decay. The front-door mat is a good place, too.

Let's not be forgetful of their role as guard dogs. This is schizophrenic in the extreme. That labradors make good guard dogs is a wicked lie. Cars, for reasons known only to canine minds, are friends – the occupants are treated to a rapturous welcome, are dragged out and licked half to death before being escorted on the grand garden tour.

Visitors on foot, on the other hand, are the enemy.

They must be galloped at, threatened with hackles on end, treated to savage barking and thrashing tails (which beheads the perennials) . . .

Guarding the garden properly requires a good deal of shuteye. Barrows must be wheeled around canine corpses on guard duty; pots, tools and trays of plants lifted over them. To disturb rabbit-filled dreams is not on. However, should a sleepy eye, half-cocked, catch the glimpse of a rabbit, the devastation of another flowerbed is inevitable. Action is decisive as a six-stone hulk crashes into the flowers. It emerges triumphant five minutes later with madly wagging tail, the corpse of a rabbit and the stalks of my best delphiniums in its jaws.

Labradors are never greater pests than when they are terrorising other poor animals which have the misfortune to call my plot home. Poultry, possums, rabbits, the peacocks and small birds are chased with deadly intent. As for the rats which lurk under the garden shed – well, what they do to them doesn't bear talking about.

Prolonged loud barking at night signals little more than absolutely nothing, accompaniment to the cattle dogs down the road or, at best, a possum in the rosebeds. The ravages inflicted by the yellow terrorists in pursuit are infinitely more terrible than that of the possum. But that is the husband's problem. He comes back to bed wet and frozen, and we are kept awake by horrible bone-crunching sounds under the bedroom window.

Any gardener knows that labradors, as well as plants, need frequent watering. During the summer months a great battle ensues between me and the dogs over ownership of the lotus and lily pond. It is a great bone of contention (excuse the pun). Spectacular labrador leaps are executed through the delicate foliage of the irises and hostas edging the pool. They plough like battleships straight through the lilies and lotus blossoms with epic splashes and crashes. I tell myself that the flowerheads skidding across the turbulent waters look very pretty. Wet-dog showers all over lady guests in pretty frocks are also in at this time of year.

An aware gardener will tell you that labradors also need mud — lots of mud; they adore it. If they find a puddle, or a patch of mud, they leap straight in, roll in it, lie in it, cooling the ancestral bellies. They are also addicted to places where something has died and is putrefying horribly. They lie on their backs in the middle, waving their legs in the air in ecstasy. They then hold competitions to see which of them can cover the verandas and their kennels with the most evil smell, or the largest amount of mud and muck. Trying to garden-train labradors is harmful to the health. It results in high blood pressure, horrible fits of rage and frustration, and coronaries.

They are out there now, those monsters with matted yellow hair, lying in wait for me on the front lawn. It is time for more garden sport. Why do I keep them? Why don't I invest in a 'Free to good home' ad in the newspaper? They are my loved companions, so help me — *Labradoricus pesticulata*, guardians of the garden.

CHAPTER TEN

THE BIG CRUNCH

It was time to tear myself away and take a break from the demon garden, the dogs and the farm, and accept an oft-extended invitation to stay with my keen gardening friend Kate. She is a fragile, feminine blonde with size 4½ feet. To my horror, I discovered that around about midnight she suffers a moon change in personality. This causes her to thrust the dainty feet into a pair of her husband's old stockman's boots and pull on a huge 'Hard Rock' shirt of her son's – skull picture on the front, motto 'Waste or be Wasted' on the back. She says these 'put her in the right mood'. She looks like a punk Minnie Mouse.

Kate presents me with a torch and invites me to go out with her. Since the farm is in the depths of the countryside, I know we are not going disco dancing. I conclude she needs company to shoot a possum or two, until she clomps off in the direction of the vege garden – without a gun.

The opossum is a small creature which, through no fault of its own, has become the enemy of Northland's forests, dairy farmers, gardeners and of all that grows. Like me, Kate has been forced to become a gardener turned hunter in a fury of rage and disbelief at the wholesale devastation the possum wreaks upon roses, shrubs and trees.

The astonishing start given to every plant in a garden by the fact that possums are buried nose to tail (position is important) beneath them is negated by the fact that possums dine only on the best – every tiny, tender new shoot that unfolds. Nightly, our dogs give warning that the creatures are leaping about, full of *joie de vivre*, holding feasts of bacchanalian proportions among (scream!) the rose shoots and fruit trees. We gardeners compare notes on the armouries of weapons, traps, cages, decline into witchcraft, nocturnal incantations and murder to which we have been driven.

On this occasion, however, Kate was stalking prey of a different type. I learn fast that I am to be an accomplice to a brutal serial killer.

'Shine that torch, here, here – no, here!' she hisses at me as she executes a wild dance that is somewhere between a Charleston and a tap dance, because of the steel-toed boots. The sounds of slaughter are horrible – *crunch, crackle, slurp* – as she crashes down on hundreds of slugs and snails along the brick paths.

I am rarely squeamish, but such grand-scale slaughter causes me to wobble the torch about. Gentle Kate is unimpressed, grabs it from me, snarls that slugs and snails are not going to get her vege garden, and that if I don't like it, to swan off and make some mugs of Milo. She says other things which cannot be repeated in a genteel publication such as this. She comes in much later, cheeks flushed and eyes shining. 'I got *hundreds*', she grins, '*and* it's good for the figure.'

So impressed am I by Kate's determination, I decide that I too have suffered the beasts' voracious appetites long enough, and must be more positive in my approach to extermination methods. I decide to begin with some in-depth reading on how the gluttonous ones shred, chop and decimate our gardens.

I discover that underneath those tentacles which go in and

out at the end of the soft foot there is a mouth-hole equipped with a thin, ribbon-like tongue called a radula. This has up to 15,000 teeth on it – a fact which leaves me wondering if we shouldn't stop complaining about the plants that get eaten but marvel that any are left at all. The book explains further that, apart from all those teeth, snails and slugs are well equipped for mass destruction because they lay eggs, hundreds and hundreds of them. They make depressions in the ground, lay bubbles of eggs, cover them with soil, and glide silently away.

When Kate had been performing her *danse macabre* it had occurred to me that since the snail can only move at a top speed of five centimetres per minute, it was sitting-duck sport. Now, armed with my new knowledge, I realise that the odds are stacked firmly in the beasts' corner, since they hold the supreme weapon – that is, more slugs and more snails, an infinite, eradicable army of tiny babies with file-like teeth, rasping away all night long while Mum potters off and lays the odd couple of hundred more eggs in between snacking.

I learn that slugs come in browns, blacks and greys, and range in size from big black monsters fifteen centimetres long to sluglings only twelve millimetres long. It appears that slugs are species of snails which lost their shells somewhere along the evolutionary line. Perhaps this is why they have few friends, because the snail does at least look presentable with its convolute, attractively marked shell. Slugs have only their repulsive fat slimy bodies, but what both pests have in common is that they are eating machines.

I read enviously that in Australia the native snail, *Strangesta capilacea*, is a carnivore, and preys upon plant-eating species, such as the introduced common humpbacked snail, so that some control over plant damage is maintained naturally. I am further depressed to learn that, even if snails are trapped somewhere where they do not have access to food, they have supernatural powers of survival. One which was mounted as an exhibit on a tablet for a number of years in the British Museum, when removed and put in tepid water, emerged from its shell and started rasping away on a cabbage leaf.

Having learned enough from this oracle, I picked out an old herbal journal in which I remember reading about the use of the slimy ones in medicine. They have been with us for a long time: Pliny the Elder (AD 33–79) suggests a dose of snails for 'Troublesome coughs', but it is important to remember 'To partake an uneven number of them'. He advocates snails boiled, raw, beaten or roasted as remedies for ailments such as swelling of the joints, corns, asthma, pleurisy and 'obstructions'. The journal recommends that, if one has a bad headache coming on, a plaster made of decapitated slugs may prove most beneficial. As late as the 1900s, in Europe, decoctions of snails, slugs and earthworms, swallowed daily, were recommended precautionary medicines against tuberculosis. One cannot be too careful.

A typical old herbal remedy reads:

> *For consumption take thirty snails, thirty slugs, and thirty earthworms of middling size. Bruise the snails, wash them and the worms in clear water. Cut the worms into pieces. Boil these in a quart of spring water and reduce to a pint. Pour it boiling on to two ounces of candied Eringoe root sliced thin. When cool, strain through a fine flannel bag. Take quarter of a pint of it warm with an equal quantity of cow's milk at twilight. Continue till well.*

Or dead?

The use of slugs and snails as dietary delicacies so impressed a Roman nobleman called Fulvius Hirpinus that he kept a snail farm, a 'cochlearia', at Tarquinium about 50 BC. The snails were fed on wine and meal, and were noted for their size and 'nobility'. Snail farms are very much with us today too, since most of those juicy creatures presented in pools of garlic butter in smart restaurants are especially cultivated.

If you are into 'natural' and 'alternative' food sources, it is not a good idea to rush out into the garden and gather a pan of snails. Unless they have been bran-meal fed, they will be poisonous, and the family would probably prefer a pan of stir-fried veges anyway (should you be so lucky as to have any left).

The more I read, the less I find myself on the side of the natural slug and snail traps such as bottles of stale beer, saucers of milk, piles of salt, eggshells and turned-down citrus-fruit shells with which I have messed about for years. As mine is an organic vege plot, and I do not care to use toxic pellets which despatch birds, hedgehogs and often domestic pets, I decide it is a garden at risk, and close the herbal journal on a prayer from the holy martyr, Trypho of Lamsacus (10th century AD). It reads:

> *Oh ye caterpillars, snails, slugs . . . I charge you by the many eyed Cherubim . . . the six winged Seraphim, . . . by all the holy Angels, the Supreme Powers . . . [etc., etc.,] hurt not the vines, nor the land, nor the fruit of the trees, nor the vegetables of the servant of the Lord, but depart into the wild mountains, into the unfruitful woods, in which God hath given you your daily food . . .'*

Some chance. I have read enough. I find myself absolutely on the side of Kate's unmitigated violence, and prepare for positive action. It is time to kit myself out with serial killer gear as fetching as hers. Now, where did I see those old Doc Marten boots of my daughter's?

> *On every stem, on every leaf . . . and at the root of everything that grew, was a professional specialist in the shape of a grub, caterpillar, aphids, or other expert whose business it was to devour that particular plant . . .*
>
> Oliver Wendell Holmes

CHAPTER ELEVEN

CALF PADDOCK
TO TREE LAWN

Leaving the animals to their business and having finished the Elizabethan Garden, I turned my attention to preparing the garden for the wedding of another blissful bride. This one attempted to squash some sixty guest onto the small front lawn, a factor which determined the garden area I was going to tackle next.

I had had a ball digging and cramming the gardens around the house with old-fashioned roses and perennials — Sissinghurst would have been impressed with my slavish devotion to Vita's 'Cram, cram, and cram' planting of the beds — but at the back of my mind was the certainty that I should, as every gardening oracle commanded, be planting trees and large shrubs to create a solid framework, the 'bones' or foundation of the garden.

We had a rose walk, a madly romantic Elizabethan Garden and an arbour for the brides to waft by and be photographed in; now we needed a large expanse of lawn for their ceremonies. The garden needed a sheltering framework of trees. Never was there a landscaper of more genius than I — why not kill two garden concepts with one inspiration? Why not create a large tree lawn?

I set my sights on the calf-rearing paddock of inverted 'V'

shape in front of the house, the perfect site for a sweeping expanse of tranquil green. Covetously studying its length, which narrowed to a triangular point, I realised that the siting of an ornamental gazebo in this furthest point would create the focal point for a perfect axis and long vista between the house and lawn-to-be.

A gazebo; this would have to come later, much later, the icing on the cake. First I had to sell the husband the brilliant idea of converting his calf pasture to tree lawn. As though this were not problem enough, the proposed new front lawn and the top of the calf paddock were bisected by an evil-smelling, muddy corridor – the channel where the cattle crossed from one side of the farm to the other. Brian would also have to be presented with the logistical problem of re-routing the cattle around rather than across the farm.

The strategy, my takeover bid, my squat, began. I dragged barrows and heavy tools through the waist-high pasture, leaving them lying nonchalantly around the paddock, which was filled with curious mounds, lumps and bumps. It says much for Brian's generosity and good humour when, having chosen my moment and presented him with the landscaping blueprint, he conceded to both demands with only mild apoplexy.

At this stage, being the newest and greenest of 'Pommie cockies', we had the great good fortune to find a treasure of a helper in a retired farmer called Harold. He took our farming education in hand, having behind him a lifetime of the sort of learning that the average Kiwi male has acquired by the age of three. With immense patience, he would listen to plans for our next project, and then tell us with great tact why it wouldn't work like that, but didn't we think it might be a good idea to do it this way, or that way? He would have made a supreme diplomat.

He and Brian took down the fences on two sides of the triangular calf paddock, began shifting gates to re-route the passage of the cattle, and left me to it.

There can be few tasks more daunting than transforming a wilderness with roller-coaster contours to the velvet lawns, complete with gracious trees, which existed in my imagination. Unfortunately, I wasn't daunted enough.

The lawn I envisaged would have been revered in front of an English stately home. The reality was jungle of kikuyu with tentacles as thick as young bamboo, which rampaged up and down the hillocks, trying to strangulate the giant tufts of paspalum grass and other noxious weeds in its path.

Fired with all the zeal of a pioneer given her first land grant, I hacked my way into the interior. The strange mounds, I decided, must be piles of rich topsoil dumped there when the excavations for re-siting the house were dug. They weren't. At the end of day one, I'd made acquaintance with the fact that they were heaps of rubbish dating from the fifties, roped together with giant kikuyu roots.

I dragged out old bicycle frames, endless metres of barbed and fencing wire, old pots, pans, buckets, shoes, clothes, bottles, heaps of unidentifiable bits from defunct farm machinery, cans, even an old gas cooker with claw feet, and a fridge . . . and more, much, much more. In the levelling of all those mounds, the only items I found which were of any use were a large quantity of old bricks which must have once been an outdoor privy.

We had no truck or utility vehicle at this time, and poor Brian would find the back of his estate car groaning each morning under the weight of my latest mound excavation. He would have to drive this into town and dump it at the tip before going to work.

Suffice it to say that by the time I had levelled that paddock, even the blisters on my callouses were blistered.

The great day finally came when I was able to take the mower into the interior. Even on its highest setting, it choked and smoked on the vicious web of kikuyu. After mowing on each of the six blade levels, even my faith that something remotely resembling a lawn was emerging was foundering. I had an area of unsurpassed ugliness, snarled with the bleached hair of the lowest layers of kikuyu, which hadn't seen the light of day in decades, and punctuated by dozens of bald spots where I had levelled the mounds. Harold and Brian, impressed with the feral nature of my new lawn, offered to 'turn the cattle in there.'

I had also discovered that the wind racing up from the swamp screamed across the piebald 'lawn' with force sufficient to hurl ropes of kikuyu into the air. I would have to put in hardy shelter trees before I could plant the exotics that grew so well in my mind's eye. I purchased six *Cupressus glabra* 'Golden Pyramid', a fast-growing, wind-hardy conifer with dense yellow foliage, which would provide winter colour when the deciduous exotics shed their leaves.

About now I embarked upon the era of the 'Three Great Truths'.

I began digging holes, and perceived the First Great Truth. Beneath a scant foot of topsoil, robbed of any nutrients by rank pasture grass, lurked a solid pan of impermeable orange clay. As I chipped and hacked, I realised that the era of The Great Dig for the beds around the house, the Elizabethan Garden and the Brides Walk had lulled me into a false sense of security. The unyielding clay in those areas had been broken up by the machinery levelling them for the re-siting of the house, so subsequent digging had been fairly easy.

The Second Great Truth entered my soul; this chipping and hacking was merely an initiation ceremony. From this day forward every plant I put into this new garden would require a planting hole twice the size of that dug in ordinary soil, and would be a crowbar and pickaxe job.

The education of the amateur gardener continued. The clay had to be attacked with elbow-shattering force to spear it open, to allow organic matter to be rammed in. It came to my attention that when it rained, the hard-won holes filled with water which did not drain away – the Third Great Truth. The labels on the conifers muttered about 'good drainage'. Commonsense told me that bog plants would not look right on the proposed tree lawn. I hacked the holes bigger.

Seeing me emerging weary and orange-streaked from the latest of my claggy pits one day, Harold, taking pity, broke the bases with a pickaxe and taught me how to provide drainage with layers of small stones, scoria and coarse sand.

The insertion of every plant in the soil became a major victory. The conifers were in, the greedy fingers of the kikuyu soon smothered the piebald patches, and after repeated close shaves by the mower, something like a lawn area began to emerge. It still had 'interesting contours' but the groundsmen at Lords couldn't have been prouder of their green than I. It was, I told myself, fit for a wedding ceremony any day.

CHAPTER TWELVE

PLANTING THE
TREE LAWN

Even as the most amateur of gardeners, I have always been of the opinion that calm, unbroken expanses of lawn are vital to the balance of the garden. They also provide the link between the house and planted beds so that each becomes part of a harmonious whole. Cool, uncluttered sweeps of green are also essential for the sense of restfulness and tranquillity which are essential components of any garden. I am unsettled when I see a large and lovely lawn bisected by fussy little beds which are invariably geometric in shape.

Since all the front windows and verandas looked out across the new expanse of 'lawn', I decided to plant all my trees in groups to the left, opposite the drive, leaving the entire centre a large unbroken expanse. The holes had been all but dynamited from the clay, and planting began – a great day.

I am fond of gold and mahogany plantings, and against the sheltering backdrop of the large conifers in went *Prunus cerasifera* 'Nigra', giving dainty pink blossoms in winter when its purple-black leaves are shed. I grouped several *Cotinus coggygria* 'Royal Purple' nearby. This shrub has wonderful grape-red foliage and carries panicles of greyish pink wispy flowers which look like puffs of smoke in mid-summer. *Berberis thunbergii* 'Atropurpureum' completed the mahogany theme, and both this shrub and the *Cotinus* look as though a pyromaniac has lit a fire in their hearts when they burst into flames of gold, orange and scarlet in autumn.

Against the frame of smouldering red-blacks I grouped several *Robinia pseudoacacia* 'Frisia', their butter-gold leaves the perfect foil for the port-wine foliage of their neighbours.

Pyrus salicifolia 'Pendula', one of my favourite trees, cools these warm colours with foliage which weeps in a silver waterfall. This tree is especially lovely when gilded with frost or moonlight. Further silver plantings have included a blue spruce, *Picea pungens* 'Koster', a slow-growing grafted variety with intense silver-blue foliage which is delightfully soft to the touch. This gem 'kost' so much, the family, clubbing together to present it to me for Christmas, renamed it 'Mum's kosterlot'. And a very handsome specimen it is, too.

Final touches of gold were provided by plantings of golden elder and ash. The former provides rich butter-yellow foliage and clusters of tiny lacey flowers, which leave bunches of shiny red-black elderberries, much loved by the birds and used extensively in European countries for the making of wines and preserves. The golden ash, *Fraxinus excelsior* 'Jaspidea', is excellent for winter colour and interest. When it has shed its leaves the ochre-yellow branches, punctuated by shiny black leaf buds, glow on gloomy days.

A weeping cedar, *Cedrus deodara* 'Golden Horizon', a grafted variety with pendulous, arching branches, completed the gold, silver and mahogany theme.

The largest of the trees on the lawn is the quick-growing *Paulownia tomentosa*, the 'foxglove tree', which is attractive at all stages of the season. Huge racemes of lavender foxglove flowers with speckled throats are hung from the bare branches in winter, making a great haze of lilac-lazuli which enchants me anew every year. This floral fiesta leaves behind bronze-coloured seedpods which decorate the tree for months after the large, handsome, heart-shaped leaves appear.

Smaller tree plantings include two of the hardier species of maples, *Acer palmatum* 'Senkaki' and *A.p.* 'Atropurpureum'. Their delicate palmate leaves, which give jewelled displays of colour in spring and autumn, do require some shelter from wind. *A.p.* 'Senkaki', the coral-stemmed maple, has branches and twigs of polished red in winter, and those of *A.p.* 'Atropurpureum' glow darkly maroon.

A dogwood, *Cornus florida* 'Rainbow', is another favourite small tree. Compact and rounded in habit, it bears a profusion of creamy white bract flowers in spring, which are followed in summer by highly ornamental foliage of green margined with yellow. This changes to intense scarlet in autumn.

No tree lawn would be complete without the true aristocrats of winter, the magnolias. Into most carefully prepared holes, wrenched from the demon clay, went *Magnolia denudata*, *M. liliflora* 'Nigra', *M.* 'Star Wars' and the star magnolia, *M. stellata*. Of the four, I believe *M. denudata*, a native of central China, to be one of the world's most beautiful flowering trees. The blooms are classical creamy white, intensely fragrant, and sit on the bare branches like great pearly tulips. This tree, underplanted with scented 'paperwhite' narcissi and forget-me-nots, is an immensely beautiful sight in late winter and early spring.

M. 'Star Wars', an Oz Blumhardt hybrid, provides drama with enormous rosy pink pointed flowers like shooting stars. The port-wine goblets of the low-growing *M.l.* 'Nigra' complement these giant blooms, and *M. stellata*'s delicate spidery flowers of creamy pink provide the perfect foil to the opulence of the other magnolias.

In all this planting I hasten to add that I did not forget what was to become very much part of my gardening philosophy –

the integration of natives with exotics, so that one does not forget that this is very much a New Zealand garden. I planted a group of the attractive small tree *Hoheria populnea* 'Alba Variegata', the native lacebark. This tree rejoices in foliage of deep green, prominently margined with cream, and bears showy clusters of white starry flowers in late summer. It looks particularly attractive against the dark background of totara groves in the paddocks beyond.

The strong, sword-like leaves of our unique cabbage trees, *Cordyline* species, give most effective contrast of foliage colour and form against the more rounded shapes of the exotics. I am particularly fond of the striking purple-bronze *Cordyline* 'Purple Tower,' and of the attractive cream, salmon and green-margined 'Albertii'. Both look excellent underplanted with *Pittosporum tenuifolium* 'Irene Patterson', which has foliage that is almost completely white when new, on slender black stems. The leaves fade to marbled pale green when mature.

The native coprosmas also give excellent service as foreground plantings. *C. repens* 'Pink Splendour' is especially attractive in winter, with glossy, deep green foliage margined yellow with wine-red highlights and softly suffused with pink. *C. repens variegata* is a versatile shrub giving attractive glossy leaves of green and cream in situations wherever variegated foliage is required.

The tree lawn was filling up rapidly, and like all amateur gardeners at this point, I was trying to brainwash myself into accepting that all the trees planted so far would, one day, really grow to the proportions bragged about on their planter labels.

I had room for about four more trees, but with the indefatigable defiance of the novice, I managed to make it five. I had seen the tuis brawling among the carmine-red bells of *Prunus campanulata* and couldn't live without this specimen. My grand finale came with the silver birches. The completion of the tree lawn coincided with the year of our silver wedding anniversary, so at its heart I planted an arbour of four *Betula pendula* 'Tristis'. These are tall, slender trees, with graceful weeping branches and twigs, heart-shaped foliage and bark beautifully marked in silvery grey. Brian and I love to sit beneath this canopy of delicate foliage and contemplate the next twenty-five years!

I planted bluebells and English primroses at their feet, perhaps with a little nostagia for the gardens of my childhood. Whatever the reason, the combination of their fragile blue and lemon flowers in spring is enchanting.

I have underplanted all the trees and shrubs with camellias and massed bulbs. I hope presently to incorporate some wildflower plantings here, too. During the period when the bulbs are in bloom, I leave the section of lawn beneath the trees unmown. I enjoy the interesting textural relief the area makes against the smooth expanse of the rest of the lawn.

There were many more luscious specimen trees I should have liked to include in the planting of the lawn, but in subsequent years I have managed to incorporate them in other planting schemes around the farm. I should have loved to have had the magnificent spectacle given by rhododendron and azalea flowers beneath my trees in spring, but for them, the largest holes packed with peat goodies and drainage materials still become coffins of brutish clay. The camellias cope – just – but the rhodos simply won't have it.

My tree lawn had been hard won, a year of backbreaking labour with crowbar and pickaxe, the hauling of infinite barrowloads of rubbish wrestled from the mounds, of drainage and organic materials, and the endless hacking of *holes*. But I was there, at the point when that icing on the cake could be mine. I spent hours designing romantic gazebos to provide the pièce de résistance. Brian and Harold looked over the building blueprints, modified their more fancy embellishments, and built me a delightful small house of trellis.

Sited carefully at the foot of the large expanse of lawn, the gazebo creates a long vista between itself and the century-old kauri homestead. Decorated in white and the same dark blues and greys of the house, a sense of unity between the two is maintained. Old roses 'Buff Beauty' and 'Sombreuil', planted to ramble over the exterior, 'rooted' the new structure to the lawn, and provided it with the aged look it required to harmonise with the house.

Today, just four years on, the trees are gaining stature and blooming well. With frequent mowing, the all-kikuyu and paspalum lawn is comfortable and presentable. It has a life of its own.

This tree lawn plays host to bridal ceremonies and parties, picnics, charity events and garden safaris. Santa Claus has been known to arrive here on a farmbike for children's Christmas parties, at which sausages sizzle. Dogs hurtle after sticks, balls and rabbits here, or it becomes a stately walk for peacocks and a playground for illegal immigrant poultry. It does not present its public with a velvet face, but with a cheerful springy carpet which does not flinch beneath the skidding claws of canines, the scraping of chairs of wedding guests, or the pounding of childish feet racing in pursuit of cricket balls and footballs.

In summer the trees provide shade and shelter, and home to all who dwell therein. In autumn its green slopes provide the stage for a theatrical display of jewelled foliage colour. Its depths provide the cradle for the trees' great roots, and the womb for the massed bulbs which emerge with such gaiety and bravery to colour the iron days of winter.

It is much used, this hard-won tree lawn. It is much loved.

GARDENER, GARDENER, SPARE THAT TREE!

The only other trees standing in the paddocks in which the homestead had been relocated were a large kahikatea, an attractive Mexican pine and a gnarled old plum.

I loved the rough, broken, reddish bark, silver-green weeping needles, clustered cones and creamy 'candle' flowers produced by the pine, a gift for every season, but it stood in a prime garden position to the right of the front lawn, and was rapidly outgrowing its situation. As it was of the variety which has a rounded head rather than soaring, upright growth, other gardeners told me it would bear careful shaping and pruning.

At this time, Harold was convalescing after hip-replacement surgery, and we had another farm helper, a cheerful, elderly fellow called Jim. I will tackle most things, but Brian had forbidden me the chainsaw, and the pine was in any case well above my reach, so I asked Jim to trim it carefully. He assured me he knew all about pruning, and had 'whacked a few back in his time'. Though this didn't exactly concur with my idea of pruning, I had no option but to leave him to it, repeating the instructions to 'shape it lightly and carefully'.

As ill luck would have it, I was called away unexpectedly, so could not keep an eye on things. On my return, Ye Gods,

Jim had massacred the tree, taking out its whole head, and had cut the branches back so savagely that only old, dead wood remained. The 'pruning' was also extremely lopsided. An hour earlier, I had had a beautiful tree; now I had a stricken mess of stark branches. The grand tantrum I threw sent Jim scurrying to the remote outposts of the farm, and impressed the husband even after twenty-five years of marriage.

I grieved and could scarcely bear to look upon the mutilated stumps. My best gardening friend, on visiting, breathed a reverent 'Oh, my God' and muttered something about scrambling a good rampant climber over it. This provided an excuse to buy the creamy white, scented wisteria, *W. venusta*, which had tempted me sorely on my last visit to the garden centre. I planted it at the foot of the stricken tree, with generous amounts of compost and 'Liquid Rain'. Venusta means handsome or charming, and so it was, its foliage divided into nine to thirteen leaflets, and covered with conspicuous silky hairs. This silky wisteria's curly tendrils soon romped up over the head of the tree, and all was well until autumn when it shed its leaves, exposing the pine's chopped stumps again.

Knowledgeable friends told me firmly that the tree would never recover, that chainsaw, stump killer and replant were the only answer. I left the pine all winter long to allow for any regrowth the following spring. A few brave, lopsided tufts of needles appeared on one side, and it seemed the moment of truth had come.

Half-heartedly reading up on evergreen climbers, I found her – *Rosa sinica alba*, alias *Rosa* 'Laevigata', who splashed great creamy white flowers bossed with golden stamens across the page, and she was *evergreen*! I learned that she smelled of cloves, and was one of the first Asiatic roses to having been introduced to England, arriving in one of the English East India ships as early as 1696.

This rose was an old favourite in the colonial gardens of New Zealand, its cuttings having been given precious space in the belongings of the pioneers as they travelled to make new lives in places desperately remote from their homelands. The rose had become naturalised in the Southern States of America, where the Cherokee maidens used to decorate their hair and feasting vessels with its blooms, hence its other name, 'The Cherokee Rose'.

Off to the nursery (again) to avail me of this beauty of chequered origin, and in she went. The shattered limbs of the pine now rejoice in a deliciously scented cascading canopy of rose and wisteria blooms, making it a much photographed sight by garden visitors in spring. When the leaves of *W. venusta* turn to gold and fall, the dense, glossy foliage of *Rosa* 'Laevigata' remains.

Jim is still with us (pruning of *any* description no longer included in his duties) and this spring, seeing me gazing up into the scented racemes of the creamy wisteria, he picked a few of the paper-white narcissi I have planted at the foot of the tree, handed them to me with a grin, and said, 'A right lovely job you've made of that scruffy old tree, Di . . .'.

The second of the trees, the old kahikatea which stood at the beginning of the rose trellis, caused us some headscratching. Previous residents had lopped off all its lower branches to a height of about twelve metres, to make what must have been a climb for children. I like to think that the mutilation had given them happy memories of garden play, but the poor tree in this state was not an asset. Its great roots had also robbed the ground for metres around of all fertility, and even the weeds which grew there were wimpish.

We could not bear to have it felled; its head above the stumps was beautiful and gave shade, shelter and food to kereru, the precious native pigeons. Like the shattered pine, the answer was to clothe it, and to this end I set about scrounging up soil, compost, manure, anything I could get my hands on, to build up a base in which I might plant climbers. I thought pink and white clematis would mingle beautifully with the tree's silvery green, needle-like foliage.

I looked up hardy varieties in my reference books; *Clematis montana* 'Alba' and *C.m.* 'Rubens' were recommended, together with *C. spoonerii* 'Snowflake'. The subsequent visit to the garden centre left me pining for the handsome *C.* 'Henryii', creamy white with dark brown stamens. What an irresistible combination it would make, threaded through the old climbing rose 'Buff Beauty'. *C. jackmanii* 'Superba' beckoned with deep velvety purple blooms some fifteen centimetres across – just begging to weave its way through old roses of lavender and purple – 'Reine des Violettes' or 'Veilchenblau'. With admirable self-restraint I told myself such hybridised beauties would wilt straight off at the mere sight of the inhospitable position under the kahikatea, and bought the stoic 'Alba' and 'Rubens'.

The reclamation area received them, and I mulched their feet well, following the rule for happy clematis – 'heads in the sun and feet in the shade'. They thrived and, two years on, have scrambled way up into the tree, cloaking the climbing stumps with great veils of pink and white stars which sway in the breeze. In winter the thick tangle of the clematis's interwined stems still cloak the trunk, attractive in their gnarled and twisted bareness.

The kahikatea stood at the beginning of the Brides Walk, so when I had managed to build up a bed of more hospitable soil beneath its feet, the obvious choice for a lusty, scrambling rose had to be 'Wedding Day'. And scramble she does, replacing the stars of 'Alba' and 'Rubens' with extravagant clusters of milky white blooms bossed with stamens of gold. Edward Lytton, an English earl writing in the last century, lauds her beauty with phrases more succinct than any I might find:

*Thro' twilight pale she climb'd and climb'd and peeped into
the dim nest of the nightingale.*

Although she blooms only once, 'Wedding Day' gives her all in
December and January, which is the favourite time for garden
weddings. The bridal couples pose for photographs beneath her.
How lovely they are, all three! There is little to be done about
pruning a rose which attains such giddy heights, so all winter
long she adorns her host with massed bunches of glowing coral
hips. I should not like to be without her.

To shade her feet, and the roots of the clematis, I planted
hardy, drought-resistant plants with silvery foliage – *Artemisia*
and the dainty *Convolvulus cneorum*. The wide-open white blooms
and silky silver foliage of the latter are a perfect companion for
'Wedding Day'. These hardy plants take little moisture from the
soil, leaving it for the beauties which soar above their heads.

I do not think that I should ever have made a huge mutilated
kahikatea the centre of a flowerbed by choice, but how glad I
am that I had to!

We had fenced off the area of paddock behind the tree for
an orchard area, and standing therein was the ancient gnarled
plum. It still managed to blossom a little in spring, though no
fruit was forthcoming. It was the perfect frame for the historic
climber *Rosa* 'Lamarque', who smothers herself in fountains of
nodding blossoms, very double and flat, with quilled and
quartered petals that on opening are a fresh lemon-white,
changing to pure white. Her scent is exquisite, the true old Tea,
and her foliage is dark, shining green. A second flush of flowers
is given in autumn. 'Lamarque' does not grow tall enough to
peep into the nightingale's nest, but she is perhaps at her most
beautiful on moonlit summer evenings, when one is in danger
of being bewitched by her perfume and porcelain blooms.

I am immensely saddened when I see old trees in the garden
situation falling victim to the chainsaw. Provided they are not

unsafe, they are a cause for rejoicing. Like walls, they are there to be clothed, to be used as mannequins for plant raiment and maquillage, such as the trees at Sissinghurst in spring. From the hair of the ancient apple trees in the orchard garden there, cascades of old roses tumble to thousands of narcissi, daffodils, bluebells, fritillarias, primroses and wildflowers at their feet. I was fortunate enough to visit Sissinghurst at this time, and it was a sight forever to be cherished in memory. It is a sight I can recreate on my own small scale here at Valley Homestead, and which you may too, no matter where your plot is, or how big or small it might be. So, 'Gardener, gardener, spare that tree!'

Happiness is a bare black stump showing a speck of green . . .

Pam Brown (1928 –)

CHAPTER FOURTEEN

THE ACER
GARDEN

Behind the rose and clematis-clad kahikatea stood the only well-sheltered spot on my entire garden-landscaping blueprint. During the happy forays to nurseries to buy old roses for the Elizabethan Garden and rose walk, another lust had been conceived in my matronly bosom – for those small trees with exquisite foliage, the maples. Their main requirement was dappled shade and shelter from harsh sun and wind, so I was extremely fortunate in having this small area.

The beauty of that maple foliage was costly, and their variety all too tempting, so my 'lust list' grew longer with every visit. 'It's called greed,' I would tell myself, as I crossed two specimens off the top and added four to the bottom. My garden-making budget would elasticise no further – I would throw myself on the mercy of the family. Like most gardeners, I am the easiest of persons to buy gifts for. At Christmas and birthday time, they have only to consult my hint, hint, clue, clue, list of 'Plants I can't live without' on the fridge door, nip down to the garden centre and make one happy Mum.

My list of 'Acers, wanted' superseded all others, and in the last four years I have been gifted with a collection which gives the small garden unparalleled effects of foliage, form and colour, especially in spring and autumn. Some of the dwarf trees have tongue-twisting names they really don't deserve, like *Acer palmatum linearilobum* 'Atrolineare' or 'Aka shigitatsu sawa', which are impossible to remember for more than ten seconds, so they are largely referred to by the more prosaic names of their donors – 'Brian', 'Sarah', 'Roger and Jean,' etc.

The area for the garden was fifteen metres by eight, sheltered by the kahikatea and by a stand of totara in the paddock behind. Though the latter are a blessing because they protect the homestead from the worst of the southwesterlies, they have a darkening effect, so I planted two *Robinia pseudoacacia* 'Frisia' and the taller-growing *Acer negundo* 'Kelly's Gold' to give the small garden a framework with warmth of colour.

Digging holes for the trees was not the Herculean task of that on the tree lawn. The soil in this area, though clay, had been penetrated and broken up by the trees' great roots. The task here was to enrich the starved soil and group my small trees where the roots would allow me to dig.

The years we lived in Asia left me with a love of all things oriental, and this was to influence my garden landscaping a good deal. Dwarf trees bring to mind for most of us the subtle and serene gardens of China and Japan. The Asians regard man as part of nature, not separate from it and, still less, superior to it. They seek harmony with nature through simplicity of design, and their gardens are planned to create moods of rest and peace of mind.

It is this simplicity and tranquillity which make oriental gardens so appealing to the Western eye. A large population reduces garden space to a premium, so the spiritual wellbeing given by such gardens is of immense value. Every element is selected and placed with extreme care. Rocks, stones and water are of equal importance to foliage shape, form and colour. Flowers are added with restricted planting of cherry blossoms, and perhaps a few azaleas. I don't know how Asians feel about our gardens crammed to bursting and planted in riots of colour.

It was my aim to maintain this simplicity of design. To incorporate the elements of stone and water, I laid a stepping-stone path leading to a small, still pool. This was made easily and quickly, because I was fortunate enough to find a preformed fibreglass shape costing only a few dollars at a garage sale.

Its rather startling swimming-pool blue colour was masked quickly by a sheet of thick polythene, the edges concealed with attractive stones from the paddocks. I fringed the pool with the ground-hugging silver-blue *Juniper squamata* 'Blue Star'. The texture of its foliage makes an appealing contrast with the delicate leaves of the maples, and a good colour foil with the larger golden *Robinia*.

I confined the roots of *Bambusa gracilis*, the fairy bamboo, in a strong pot and sank it behind the pool where it arches prettily. Though the basic landscaping elements were complete, I could not resist blueing a generous gift token on a stunning oriental lacquer pot to stand at the end of the garden. If an Asian garden is so small that there is no room for water, it is customary to incorporate a pot such as this in the design, fill it was water, and float a few beautiful blooms on the surface. The garden centre had some rather fetching stone lanterns and pagodas too, but upon reflection, I decided they smacked of Japanese gnomery and left them there.

The simple landscaping complete, the collection of the dwarf trees began. It is a difficult task to list the most beautiful of the acers, but I will try.

Among the upright varieties, *Acer palmatum* 'Burgundy Lace' (which needs no further descriptive words from me) and *A.p.* 'Katsura' are the colour stars of the seasons. 'Katsura' comes into leaf with foliage as pale as the spring sunlight. It changes to a fiesta of orange-reds, as though the tree had gone straight from spring by continually arriving new golden leaves which finally revert back to an explosion of orange-reds in autumn. *A. p.* 'Burgundy Lace' exchanges its leaves in late summer for those of intense scarlet, making it look from afar as though every leaf were a flower.

Acer palmatum linearilobum 'Atrolineare' (alias 'Sarah') has the narrowest leaves imaginable – five deeply lobed, narrow 'fingers' form the entire leaf. Foliage is black-red in spring, paling to bronze-green later, before becoming searing crimson in autumn. This small tree creates shadowed leaf patterns which have a mystical, oriental effect in their beauty which I find intriguing.

A. p. 'Osakazuki' is called the 'fire leaf maple' for its scarlet and crimson foliage in autumn. Its form, which is round and wide-spreading, creates a perfect balance with the more upright trees. The foliage of 'Osakazuki' is rich green in summer, and the tree has the added bonus of bearing ornamental red-winged seeds.

For stunning colour contrast with its companions, *A.p.* 'Ukigumo' is a favourite. Leaves of palest green are marbled and flecked with a blend of white and pink, the rosy markings becoming more dominant in spring and autumn. The tree is small and slow growing, gradually building up into an upright, twiggy form. Because of the delicacy of its colouring it is called the floating clouds maple – who could resist such temptation?

To complement the robinias and tall maple 'Kelly's Gold', and to incorporate mellow foliage among the other maples, I chose *A.p.* 'Aureum', which has the bonus of growing slightly taller, giving a variation and balance in height among the dwarf trees. Its growth habit is upright, bushy and twiggy. The new spring growth is deep yellow, often tinted pink at the margins, gradually changing to soft lime-green in summer, and to old gold in autumn.

Among the oh-so-elegant weeping maples, *A.p. dissectum* 'Crimson Queen' gives a waterfall of finely dissected crimson foliage, and 'Viridis' is a perfect foil for her, weeping finely textured feathery leaves of jade-green which turn yellow and orange in autumn. 'Red Dragon' is similar in form to 'Crimson Queen' but has a faster growth habit, and soon forms a beautiful cascading mound of deep purplish red foliage, which deepens to scarlet in autumn.

Soon I had room for only one more dwarf tree, and *A. p. d.* 'Garnet' proved irresistible. Mound-shaped, it weeps long cascading branches of deeply dissected leaves with the colour of a garnet gemstone's reddish orange fire.

In return for this foliage fiesta and beauty of form, the small trees ask only for shelter from burning winds and strong sunlight, and a cool, moist root-run. Who would not gladly oblige them thus?

The oriental garden thus planted, I set my sights on covering the ground with small rocks or pebbles, but these proved too expensive for the almost empty coffers of the garden-making budget at this time. I settled for a groundcovering of fine bark chippings, which was a natural material and which would also maintain a cool root run. As all the trees were deciduous, the small garden looked a little forlorn in winter, so I underplanted them with the groundcover *Pratia puberula*.

This creeping plant has a dense network of small foliage, and smothers itself with tiny blue star-like flowers almost throughout the year in Northland. These form a carpet of blue which is not intrusive enough to detract from the beauty of the trees in other seasons but enhances them and gives interest when they shed their leaves. The overall effect is so attractive, the expensive pebbles are no longer yearned for. One word of warning, however. *Pratia puberula* is a creeping groundcover, and can be invasive in other situations such as rock gardens or borders.

The small garden was complete and the trees in position, but I felt it needed an edging of some kind to enclose the bark chippings and to divide it from the lawn of the orchard area.

Nothing manmade would harmonise with the natural elements of bark, stone and water. Wood was the answer, preferably aged, and I knew just the thing!

Roots from the great kauri trees which once covered the Hikurangi swamp, below our gardens, continually work their way to the surface of the pasture. The farmers grazing the land are only too happy to have them removed. There followed a period of car abuse when the husband was not around, as I loaded it with choice lengths of gnarled wood thousands of years old. They mark the confines of the maple garden admirably, forming a harmonious whole with the other natural materials already incorporated in its design.

In autumn and spring you will find me in the *Acer* garden, away with the Floating Clouds, in the company of the Crimson Queen and Red Dragons.

CHAPTER FIFTEEN

STRICTLY FOR
THE BIRDS

This afternoon I came home from shopping to find the entire poultry population of our small farm firmly in possession of the front lawn, sunning themselves thereon.

I have only myself to blame. Like children, they know that my discipline is inconsistent, and are therefore quick to take advantage. My half-hearted 'poultry purge' one week finds them filtering nonchalantly back the next. My only excuse for such sloppy standards is the pleasure I feel in sharing the garden with a wonderful variety of native and domestic birds. When the turkey mob see 'Old Blue', the peacock, strutting importantly across the lawns, they see no reason why they should not do so too.

Unloading the groceries, I watch Old Blue clicking open the great iridescent fan of his tail, but his 'tale' is sad. His peahen, 'Plain Jane', is utterly besotted with the grotty old turkey gobbler whose blue and red head is straight from a sci-fi movie. He is in moult and looks like something the cat has dragged in. Old Blue wears himself to a frazzle, unfurling his tail in a great arc of quivering greens, electric blues, and of burnished golds which rival the sun, but the ungrateful hussy trails around with blind adoration after her unhandsome lover. Could it be, perchance, that we are going to get some 'perkies'?

Such exotic offspring would add to our other rare and eccentric breed of bird – our 'turkey-ducks'. One of the turkey hens took over a wild duck's nest in which there must have been some eggs. She incubated these with her own, and in due course came marching hungrily back into the garden with a brood of twelve turkey chicks and two little ducklings. To prevent the hawks taking them, we confined the family in a pen, until the ducklings, growing so rapidly, would uplift 'Mum' into the air when they dived under her, leaving no room for the smaller turkey chicks. We removed the ducklings to an adjacent pen, but from the moment we released them they were 'turkey-ducks' in every respect, and have never approached water. They even roost with their huge parents at night, albeit at a lower level.

All our poultry are free-range, and as far as they are concerned, this range is inclusive of the gardens whenever they can get away with it. The busy little bantam hen, emerging with a brood of tiny chicks from beneath a large daisy bush in the perennial border, is a living testimony of this. They will certainly rough up the border for a while, as she teaches them to scratch, but the bonus will be total annihilation of bugs and pests in the area.

As for the hawks, even as the shadow of their immense wingspan of dappled tans and tawny golds shadows the garden, sending all the other birds for cover, one pauses to admire their strength, and the magnificence of their soaring, swooping, plummeting flight. They have fledglings to feed, too, but I wish they did not have to dine on the doves, poultry chicks, and smaller birds. But that is, after all, the way of things.

It would be hard to imagine working in the garden without those most cheerful and constant of companions, the fantails. As I weed and prune, they chatter their approval, and play miniature hawk to the insects I disturb.

When I am getting dressed in the morning I watch the silvereyes performing amazing acrobatic feats in the fuchsia flowers under the window. They are so tiny and fragile they can almost hang suspended from the larger flowers. Their nests are awe-inspiringly beautiful structures of fine grasses and fibres, attached like a hammock with spiders' webs to twigs or leaves, on the outermost foliage of shrubs in quieter parts of the garden.

As for the thrushes and blackbirds, I must admit to having rather a love-hate relationship with them in spring, when, with nests full of hungry fledglings to feed, they follow me, uprooting seedlings, new annuals, and scooting soil all over the paths in their keen-eyed search for worms and bugs. I am exasperated but remind myself that without them I should have vast armies of slugs and snails all chomping madly away at these tender plants anyway. It is always amusing to watch the fledglings, which are as large as their parents when they leave the nest, pestering to be fed, and to observe Ma and Pa 'mock pecking' all around the ground, to teach these lazy infants to feed themselves – 'This is where the food is now, junior!'

I also admit to cursing the sparrows for cramming the climbing roses with huge untidy nests which seem to be built in minutes, and for pecking the buds off the wisteria and weeping cherries, but they too, with all their raucous squabbling, are part of this living garden tapestry.

On gloomy days of winter half light, I remind myself that it will not be long before the tuis, heralding spring, will come tumbling into the dark-rose blossoms of the early blooming *Prunus campanulata*, filling the gardens with echoing song. It is worth enduring winter to watch them falling, half-stoned, out of the kowhai trees around the pond, intoxicated by the nectar in the golden bell flowers.

Also in the winter garden, I have been stopped in my tracks by the pristine beauty of my white fantail doves, treading curiously along a path transformed by the frost into a sheet of icing-sugar sparkle.

Flashes of jewelled brilliance are given to grey days by flocks of flamboyant rosellas, perhaps those we released from the old aviary, swooping into the magnolias in a kaleidoscope of brilliant reds, emeralds, sapphires and golds.

With spring come the starlings, and each year we are amused by their eccentric and innovative choice of nesting places, though these do cause problems. Preparing to light a large brick-built barbecue for a charity lunch in the garden, Brian had just put a taper to the charcoal when an indignant starling mum erupted out of the top of the chimney, leaving a nest full of piteously squarking fledglings.

Pa starling scolded us noisily from an adjacent fence, and as a hundred or so hungry guests arrived, festivities had to be halted while a large-scale Rescue 111 programme was carried out by a visitor volunteer force. It was an extremely delicate procedure, with Brian (having unlaid the smouldering charcoal, etc.) twisting himself up into the base of the chimney and manually pushing the nest, intact with its precious cargo, further towards the top so that others could lift it out.

We put the nest into a plastic plant pot, covered it with a piece of dark cloth and hung it from the side of the barbecue. Ma starling ruffled her feathers crossly, hopped back in, and settled down to rear her young in the new abode without further ado.

A small bird we hold precious is a little female ring-necked dove, who rears regular families of fledglings in the tangle of *Jasminum polyanthum* and the old rose 'Mme Alfred Carrière', on the veranda pillar outside the kitchen window. She is a constant companion, sitting in a plant-pot nesting tray which Brian placed beneath one of her more careless 'two twigs and sit' nests. So patiently she sits for eighteen days, and so diligently she feeds and rears her young, repeating the process a number of times per year. She is a garden resident who would be sorely missed should any mishap befall her.

The only bird which brings a sadness not of its own making is our unique native pigeon, kereru. Trembling on the edge of extinction, poached by man and animal predator alike, the numbers we observe decline sharply each year. During years spent travelling the world, I have never seen a bird more gentle or more beautiful.

We have banded the native trees surrounding the garden, in the hope that those few birds that come will nest and rear young which cannot be plundered by possums or rodents. I have planted guava bushes in controlled areas, to supplement their food sources which are being destroyed by possums.

The sound of kereru tumbling into the kahikatea, puriri and taraire trees, the glimpse of their cream breasts and iridescent green heads, is an experience our children and grandchildren may never have. I fear and grieve that it will follow the path of that once most fascinating of New Zealand birds, the huia, which was shot to extinction by the 1940s.

The call of the kiwi from the bush around the garden diminishes annually, too, through predators and competition for food, factors over which we can exert only limited control. On a more cheerful note, the morepork, ruru, is a frequent visitor, swooping into the garden at dusk to sing his haunting requiem.

Crossing China on a holiday trip this year, the absence of birdlife was most conspicuous, even in remote countryside areas. The rural silence seemed heavy and unnatural, devoid of birdsong. Sadly, in a nation that must struggle to feed a billion people, there is little food for birds. They, and other animals, have become a secondary food source for people.

Here, in New Zealand, on the other side of the world, as

we leave our gardens at dusk, the last sounds we hear are the lovely liquid cadences and arpeggios of birdsong. It is the first sound we hear on waking, a sound which will continue to fill the hours of our garden labours. Each day when I wake to this bird-embroidered dawn, I known that in sharing my garden with them I am in possession of a great privilege, gifted with the perpetual pleasure of their companionship and song.

It is for reasons like these that my aspirations towards having an immaculate manicured garden will never eventuate. That feathered mob roughing up the front lawn and pecking at the perennials is in certain possession of the knowledge that this plot is strictly for the birds.

CHAPTER SIXTEEN

A FILTHY HOLE
IN THE GROUND

There was no other way to describe it; it was simply a huge, filthy hole, filled with murky water, which had been excavated between two paddocks and was perilously near the edge of the drive. Was it the brainchild of a maniac? The erosion problem it had left was nightmarish. With each good Northland rain, landslips from the paddocks above would avalanche down and a few more centimetres would crumble from the side of the drive. Tame ducks had taken over the pond and, searching for food in the luscious mud beneath the edges, had undermined these badly. The feet of the unwary, treading thereon, were plunged into the water! It was sad to see the ducks go, but kind homes were found for them.

The hole was fed by a creek from the bush; apart from a small broken drainage pipe under the drive, which allowed water to seep beneath, causing subsidence, no provision had been made for coping with high water-levels. This worried us a good deal, since the steep drive is our only vehicular access.

The banks of the pool were a jungle of rank pasture grass, ragwort and thistle. In summer the clay base cracked into leg-breaking faultlines, and in winter slipped steadily down into the water. The jungle was scattered with great chunks of clay which had been hurled up by the excavating machinery. It was different clay to the brutish orange stuff I had fought a one-woman armed combat with in the rest of the garden-making areas. When wet, these chunks had the consistency of sticky putty; when dry, they were so hard they would have done for fill for earthquake-safe buildings.

We placed a row of these clay chunks along the watery side of the drive, where they fulfilled the function of painted stones, preventing the vehicles of friends becoming amphibious on dark evenings. There was absolutely nothing one could do but hurl them into the paddocks where, in time, they became powdered by the feet of the cattle.

It was an appalling scene. I have spoken about the wilderness sight of the mountainous calf-rearing paddock in its pre-tree-lawn days, which had not daunted me. The hole in the ground daunted me. It did not engender in my bosom a stout heart of courage and valour, nor create the spirit of indomitable resolve which usually comes effortlessly to less sane gardeners. Half-hearted massacres with the weedeater across its dangerous slopes left me cowed and exhausted. Spades, grubbers and shovels, laid down for a moment, disappeared into the depths of the faultlines forever.

If the hole had one redeeming feature, this was that it was large enough to make a small ornamental lake. In my more optimistic and hallucinatory moods I tried to envisage oriental water gardens. Brian would roll his eyes heavenwards when I prattled about lotus blossoms, pagodas and bridges of Chinese-red lacquer.

It took Cyclone Bola, which stunned New Zealand with its suddenness and ferocity, to make this vision reality. In the twenty-four hours to 9 am on Monday, 7 March 1988, the cyclone swamped us with 125.3 mm of rain. This continued for another twenty-four hours, leaving a total of 302 mm (almost twelve inches), which caused the water in the hole to rise dramatically, flooding the surrounding paddocks and drive. When the waters receded, inches had crumbled from the latter, and the pond was now less than two metres away from its edge. Massive slips had fallen from the banks above the water. We were left with a disaster area, and all other farm and garden projects were halted while we prepared to deal with it.

Experts were called in. We were told that first priority was to drain the pool and insert a new concrete culvert pipe under the drive, to replace the old one beneath which the water now rushed, causing a subterranean tunnel. It was only a matter of time before this section of the drive collapsed, sealing us off from the outside world. Renewing the pipe would maintain safe water-levels under all weather conditions. We were advised to terrace the steep eroding slopes into two levels, to halt the slips from the paddocks above.

Battle commenced. We called in various contractors to give quotes; several took one look, and were never seen or heard of again. Others declared it couldn't be done, because the dangerous slopes allowed no access for machinery; the job could not be done without machinery. I brooded darkly on how our pioneer ancestors carved whole farms from the bush with less machinery than it takes us to mow a lawn. Brian spent hours draining the hole with miles of black alkathene piping so that work might commence. He crashed down the telephone after a similar 'sorry, can't do' verdict from another set of contractors, snarling to me that building a flyover from the farm to the outside world might be an easier alternative.

I continued thumbing through the yellow pages, and eventually found that rare and precious commodity, the contractor who studies the devastation with index finger on lips, whose deadpan face suddenly breaks into a huge grin. 'Mmm, she'll be tricky,' he says, followed by — as the flame of challenge leaps in his eyes – 'We'll give her a go – *no problem*!'

Enter George, Ringo and Selwyn John. George was a huge blond Viking who favoured golden ringlets, Ringo's pate was shaved bald as an egg and Selwyn John rejoiced in bird's-nest dreadlocks. The last two were massive Maoris, and all three sported a nice line in rippling singlets. They were full of youth, rude good health, strength and laughter, tossing crowbars, pickaxes and sledge-hammers about like toothpicks.

Their task was not easy. Working knee-deep in mud in kneeling and crawling positions, they re-excavated the tunnel beneath the drive for the realignment of two concrete culvert sections, each a metre in diameter. These had to be lowered either side of the drive by a pulley from the back of a truck. There was even the occasional grunting and puffing from our three amiable giants, while lifting and heaving the pipes into position.

All this heavy manual labour engendered the need for constant sustenance, and mealtimes were frequent. The appetites of George, Ringo and Selwyn John began to hold an awful fascination for me after I swore to Brian that I had seen Ringo devouring a whole leg of mutton. Each morning at 9.30 they would have breakfast – a whole sliced loaf *each*, made into sandwiches, mountains of chops, or whole chickens, five kilogram bags of apples, all washed down with an astonishing number of bottles and thermoses of tea and coffee.

Morning tea, about 11 am, saw the despatch of huge slabs of cream-filled cake, several packets of biscuits each and two-litre bottles of lemon and cherryade. Lunch at 12.30 pm repeated the breakfast menu, but might include a tray of meat pies and a stack of cooked kumara. Afternoon tea, at 3 pm, followed the same lines as morning tea, and wiped out any scraps which might somehow have been overlooked – such as the odd box of a dozen fruit pies.

The three giants were lean, hard and muscled. I used to

worry whether their wives had any of their salaries left with which to feed themselves and their children. I wondered how long it took each morning to prepare such gargantuan picnics. They deserved a medal each for services to mankind.

After the culvert was in place, a neighbouring contractor took on the vital task of building a retaining wall across the pool, two metres away from the crumbling edge of the drive. It was unenviable work; standing knee-deep in cold slime, he had to ram 2.5-metre posts of H4 double-tanalised timber to a depth of 1.5 metres. Retaining walls were then made by hammering on layers of half rounds behind the stays. Brian, Harold and I hauled rocks and topsoil from the paddocks to backfill the area behind the wall, gradually bringing it level with the drive. To see this area safely barricaded behind retaining walls brought us a considerable measure of relief.

George, Ringo and Selwyn John continued this work, gradually barricading all the banks of the pool behind further retaining walls. I presented them with two gigantic chocolate cakes and shared afternoon tea with them on their last day. The area was extremely quiet without their booming laughter and colourful cursing on the days after their departure. Filling the car with petrol at the garage a couple of months later, I nearly leapt out of my skin when a giant paw crashed down onto my shoulder with vertebrae-crushing force, and Selwyn John's huge belly laugh rumbled as he yelled, 'Them banks still holding behind our walls, lady?'

It was our turn for hard labour. Brian, Harold and I worked by hand at cutting the eroding slopes into two terraces, with spade, shovel and crowbars. Have you ever tried to wheel away a barrowload of weighty clay soil across a slippery slope on an angle of forty-five degrees? Many of the loads found their way into the water.

We cut the first terrace immediately above the stabilising walls around the waterline to create a level walkway all the way around. Life became a punishing monotony of heaving and wrestling barrows of soil off-site, and barrowloads of rocks on.

We were fortunate in having paddocks littered with rocks which would delight any garden landscaper. We did not, however, have any farm machinery, and every piece of stone had to be carried in manually. We levered them with crowbars across the pasture until they were poised on the edges of the steep banks above the terracing. Then we played 'devil's marbles', tilting them over the edge in the hope that they would come to rest on the walkway above the waterline. The colourful epithets and expletives I had learned from George, Ringo and Selwyn John roared from my lips when, having laboured hugely to roll a choice rock to the edge of the chasm, it would thunder down the slope (doing the terracing no good at all) and crash into the pool!

Years of lifting heavy items in and out of packing crates during my time as an army wife had given me a stong back, but how it stood up to the abuse I inflicted on it during those days of heaving rocks I do not know. I hope I shall not suffer too much later in life. Harold tried to teach me that there was an art, a science, in shifting heavy objects. I am certain he was right, for ancient civilisations were built by men's hands and backs alone. I tried to find the point of balance which enabled one to work with the weight of the stone, instead of against it, but I invariably ended up red-faced, sweating and using my back like a crane. He grinned at me one day as I buckled at the knees under the burden of my latest boulder, and said, 'You can shift rocks some fellows would think twice about, Di.' I think it was a compliment.

Brian, rushing home from work to put in a few hours 'hard', would find the pair of us bruised, battered, always bleeding and filthy. I crushed my fingers, my toes, my bosom and many other portions of my anatomy in those days of playing weight-lifting with rocks.

We built a waist-high stone wall above the walkway to support the second layer of terracing above. Harold taught me the basics of dry stone-walling, which the early pioneers around Whangarei had used when they built walls of stone to mark boundary lines. I learned that the rocks must be tilted slightly backwards when they are to fulfil the purpose of a retaining wall. It was lifting them into position before they were stacked which was the killer.

Rocks. We rolled, roped, lifted, barrowed, levered and carried them. My hands (which once rejoiced in fine embroidery) grew hard and strong, the knuckles thickening to a degree where I could not pass the rings of less physical days over my fingers.

Slowly the devastation area was beginning to show a pattern and take shape. At last the great day came when we could wheel barrowloads of rock right around the walkway, which speeded up the stabilisation of the slopes immensely.

Planting the new terraces before the eroding winter rains came was of vital importance, and it was already autumn, with less hours of daylight for labour. Brian spent every moment he could take away from farm and business, ramming in pegs and endless metres of wired wooden edging to retain planting lines and pockets at the base of each terrace.

Harold moved giant rocks by every method known to man, for embedding at key landscaping points on the terraces, at the behest of she-who-must-be-obeyed. She spent the days wheeling in loads of smaller rocks for backfilling, and returning the barrows of the topsoil which had been wheeled out, during the excavation of the terraces. Each barrow when emptied had to be filled with a mandatory load of clay chunks to scatter in the paddocks before it was allowed off-site. I wondered if we would finish the work before the end of the millenium, leave alone before winter.

CHAPTER SEVENTEEN

THE VISION
COMPLETE

Working at a frantic pace to beat the shortening days of autumn, we managed to complete the basic stabilisation and landscaping of the pond by early winter – optimum planting time.

Although the water gardens on the mental blueprint were to be oriental in aspect, the area was also to be my 'nativery'. The homestead luxuriated beneath lashings of old roses, perennials, lavenders and other cottage-garden 'pretties'; now I was going to go native. The framework of the gardens was to be of kowhai trees, ponga, treeferns and *Cordyline*, interspersed with a few exotics for deciduous colour, and generously underplanted with shrubs such as *Coprosma*, *Pseudopanax*, *Pittosporum*, *Phormium* and native grasses.

It seemed a final irony that the planting conditions on all three sides of the roughly circular area were totally different. The left-hand terraces were in the shadow of an enormous stand of totara and had a damp, shaded aspect. The rear area, where the creek trickled into the pond, was bog in winter and drought-stricken in summer. The high right-hand terraces stood in full sun, received the full force of the wind and offered baked clay at its most spiteful. It was also woven through with the stump and roots of an immense totara which had been felled.

These extremes in climatic and soil conditions made my planting balance difficult. It was logical to create a harmonious whole by repeated plantings of the foundation trees on all three sides. While the ponga and kowhai would thrive in the damp shade on the left terraces, they would hate the arid plains of those on the right. I considered changing the basic plantings, but realised that the extremes would affect other species in just the same way.

I had set my heart on enclosing the terraces with kowhai, and on planting ponga at lower levels, to shade the walkway around the pond. I decided the compromise was to group each in the position they would like best, unified by repeated underplantings throughout the area.

The dogs and I went bush to gather ponga, which grew on the hill in abundance. The backdrop of this small mountain of bush and the uninterrupted vistas across the pasturelands of the swamp below give me the most beautiful of settings for my gardens. On the hill we have some thirty kauri, stands of totara, kahikatea, rimu, tanekaha and other unique native trees. We have placed this bush in the care of the Queen Elizabeth II Trust, so that it might be safe in perpetuity.

Gathering ponga, I chose six small specimens, assuming they would transplant better than large ones. Some were growing in the most inhospitable of places, on outcrops of rock or clinging by two roots to sheer crumbling slopes. They would relish their damp, shady new home – I thought. They did not. Having heaved them all the way down, and planted them with love, they all expired immediately. Fearing the effect of the forthcoming winter rains on the terraces, I cut my losses and replaced them with specimens in planter bags from the nursery. Less than three years on, these have soared to a height of 1.5 metres.

The kowhai and ponga were underplanted with the New Zealand rock lily or rengarenga, *Arthropodium cirratum*, for its attractive sword-like foliage, generous panicles of white flowers and clump-forming habit. Once it is established, it self-sows and can be divided up to continue making an excellent groundcover for other areas. Hostas with gold and cream-splashed leaves made an excellent colour foil among the rengarenga.

The *Coprosma robusta* 'Williamsii Variegata' which, unlike its hardier relatives, needs a sheltered position, provides a stunning splash of weeping variegated cream and green to lighten darker corners and makes excellent underplanting.

I envisaged a seating alcove in the middle of this left-hand terrace, shaded by the lacey umbrellas of ponga. I did not dare dig out the alcove from the perilously fragile new terracing without Brian's approval. It was forthcoming, and he gave the work of excavating, and reinforcing the walls of the arbour with ponga logs, to a neighbour's teenage boys who wanted holiday jobs. I was proud of this seating-place; it was the first touch of elegance to reach the raw area, and being able to sit for 'smokos' on the bench seemed the height of civilisation after months of hard labour.

The main focal-point of the water gardens (we felt we could call them thus since the completion of the terracing and arrival of the seat) was to be a gazebo, sited in the middle of the bank immediately opposite the drive. Brian calculated the price of the materials for my design, but in the garden centre we saw a kitset building on special offer which actually cost less. It was purchased, and while I continued planting, Brian levelled the site and began trying to assemble the kitset.

We concluded after an hour that the kitset had been on special offer because the instructions for assembly belonged to another design, or had been written by a person who had never clapped eyes on this particular model. Either way, they were sanity-threatening, and he had to practically remake the whole thing to his own design.

Blood pressures plummeted when it was finally assembled, and, together with the seat, I painted it Chinese-lacquer red. We added a few embellishments of our own to give the gazebo a more oriental aspect. Brian now refers to it as my 'playhouse' because it houses my collection of bonsai or 'tortured trees', which I enjoy creating from inexpensive starter plants.

As the gazebo commanded central position, I felt it needed to be fronted by a couple of steps so that people could step down towards the water and enjoy the reflections. I was confident that the fetid murky depths which presently lurked there would one day be replaced by clear waters with lilies floating on its face. In one of the paddocks furthest from the pool there was a marvellous stone. I knew it would make the perfect step; it was slightly hollowed in the centre as though generations of feet had smoothed it. Tapering to a diamond shape underneath, it was also huge, and I still shudder to think what it weighed. I knew Brian and Harold would draw the line at this one, but I was determined to have it as the pièce de résistance in front of the gazebo.

Pigheaded, I rolled that stone six turns a day with a crowbar across the paddocks, which was all I could manage without becoming paraplegic. The journey took a fortnight. I had the stone sitting at the fenceline above the terraces – 'Oh no! No, no!' cried the two poor men involved in my landscaping escapades. I grovelled, I pleaded. They cut the wire of their newly erected fencing, then roped and crowbarred that hunk of stone into position for me. It looked fantastic! It is a monument to my foolhardiness and their long-suffering patience.

To the right of the gazebo I planted that most magnificent of trees, *Salix vitellina* 'Pendula', golden weeping willow. 'Vitellina' means 'the colour of egg yolk', and the names *Salix* alba 'Tristis' and *S. a.* 'Chrysocoma', which mean 'weeping golden hair', are both used to describe its pendulous yellow branches. Their glowing tracery against the sky, reflected in the face of the pool, brings great pleasure in winter. The tree's only fault, which must be spoken, is that it is no candidate for planting near an ornamental pool in a home-garden situation. Its rate of growth is prodigious, and in three years the mere sapling I brought home in a medium-sized planter bag has grown to a height and spread eight by eight metres. A case of, first, read the planter label, and second, believe it!

My good fortune was that the area could take, and needed, a framework of large trees. I chose the larger growing maples, *Acer negundo* 'Kelly's Gold,' and *A. n.* 'Violaceum'. The latter has ornamental new leaf shoots of violet covered in a white bloom, the former bears varying shades of gold foliage according to season. Both are deciduous, letting sunlight through in the colder months. In late winter, their bare branches are hung with a colourful display of long pendulous tassels of reddish pink flowers, which look magnificent silhouetted against the winter sky.

It was impossible to resist another planting of my favourite *Magnolia denudata*, the Yulan magnolia, to provide a background to the gazebo. Its white tulip flowers would enhance the oriental aspect of the garden, would they not? A grouping of the weeping pear, *Pyrus salicifolia* 'Pendula', and *Robinia pseudoacacia* 'Frisia' gave silver and gold foliage and completed the planting of large trees in the area. *Cordyline* 'Albertii', *C.* 'Purple Tower' and *C. banksii*, interspersed among the exotic trees, provided dramatic change of foliage form, colour and texture, and also contributed a unifying principle to the entire tree plantings.

While the planting continued, Brian was building tiers of sleeper steps to provide working and viewing access on the slopes of the terraces. The sleepers were composed of Australian hardwood, and were equally hard on chainsaw and temper.

Plantings on the damp, shady side of the pool complete, I reached the hot, dry side, where I had decided on a red, gold and grey scheme for year-round colour. The unparalleled *Leucadendron* 'Safari Sunset' provides constant coral-red flowers and its sport *L.* 'Jester' gives stunning variegated foliage of green margined with cream and salmon, in addition to rosy red blooms shaded with sunset pink. As a complete contrast in shape and form to the upright leucadendrons, I chose the weeping ornamental grass *Cortaderia* 'Gold Band'. A little on the large side for many gardens, this grass forms an architectural clump of pendulous green foliage deeply margined with gold. In autumn it throws up dramatic cream flower plumes which are most eye-catching.

Other lower-growing ornamental grasses which revel on the hot dry terraces include *Chionochloa flavicans*, which bears metre-high plumes of greenish cream, and *Carex lucida*, which gives a foil of fine hair-like coppery bronze foliage. The silver-blue grass *Festuca ovina* 'Glauca' looks wonderful planted with the lime-yellow foliage of *Coleonema* 'Sunset Gold.'

Further red tones are provided by the ever-hardy shrub *Photinia* 'Red Robin', by the handsome erect flax *Phormium* 'Guardsman', and by the lower-growing *P.* 'Maori Maiden', *P.* 'Maori Sunrise' and *P.* 'Dazzler'. *P.* 'Yellow Wave' gives handsome, semi-weeping foliage of cream and green, and *P.* 'Black Knight' makes a stunning companion plant to all yellow tones.

Dwarf conifers form softer, rounded shapes among the architectural flaxes and give year-round colour. I am particularly fond of the attractive weeping golden fronds of *Chamaecyparis pisifera* 'Filifera Aurea', but its name is something else again! I also have a soft spot for the conifer *Thuja occidentalis* 'Rheingold', which grows into a neat mound of feathery, coppery bronze foliage. *Juniperus squamata* 'Blue Star' complements the rounded conifer forms of mellow tones beautifully, giving brilliant steel-blue, low-growing foliage, which always looks crisp and clean.

An excellent small shrub I should hate to be without is *Nandina domestica* 'Pygmaea', dwarf heavenly bamboo. I am fascinated by the common name of this plant. The translation from the botanical Latin is somewhat loose, methinks, since its neat, mounded head of narrow leaves of brilliant scarlet, orange and yellow could not possibly be remotely related to any imaginable species of bamboo.

Silver tones are provided among the reds and golds with *Artemisia* species. Margery Fish stated firmly that their exuberance needed 'curbing at times since they have no respect for the privacy of others'. I was happy with such waywardness, since it helped to cover those bare terraces admirably. Mrs Fish approved, however, of the stately cardoon, *Cynara cardunculus*, which I enjoy. Its 1.5 metre tall stems of large, deeply cut, felted, silver foliage and branching, purple thistleheads make a dramatic statement wherever it is planted.

Another plant giving excellent architectural form is the native *Astelia chathamica* 'Silver Sword'. It is especially attractive after a shower of rain, when the edges of its broad leaves glisten with trembling raindrops.

The coprosmas made excellent work of providing gold and green variated foliage. *Coprosma repens* 'Pink Splendour' has spectacular foliage of glossy olive-green margined yellow, with wine-red highlights softly suffused with pink. The handsome, lobed leaves of *Pseudopanax* 'Gold Splash' completed the variegated gold and green plantings.

The terraces now had a respectable covering of trees and shrubs, but there was one more difficulty to overcome. At the end of the rugged, arid bank lay the stump and great roots of the felled totara. A number of these roots were above ground, because constant erosion had washed away the little topsoil that had once been there, leaving only a layer of white, gritty clay.

My garden-making to date had taught me that no matter how dry, wet, hot, cold or inhospitable a planting situation might be, there existed plants that would absolutely adore the spot. Also, a golden rule, which became part of my gardening philosophy very early, is 'if you can't beat it, make a focal point of it'. Nevertheless, I thought I might have met my Waterloo among the roots of the totara, until the thought of hardy succulents occurred. Kind friends provided these, and sure enough, they merely laughed at the arid desert conditions. They multiplied to give a strong, dense covering of gold, silver and bronzy pinks, which held and stabilised the bank admirably.

The emphasis on the plantings around the water gardens had been on foliage, form and colour which would look good all year round and require little maintenance, but when all the trees and shrubs fulfilling this criteria were in, the area seemed to need the softening effect of a few flowers.

I have restricted them in variety and colour to rich coral tones, to link with the strong red of the lacquer on the gazebo and seats. Deepest velvet-red New Guinea impatiens thrive and give a most pleasing splash of colour under the kowhai and ponga on the left bank. The red woolly flowers of tall, hardy *Anigozanthos* or 'kangaroo paw' distinguish the hot dry area. Clumps of the versatile daylilies, *Hemerocallis* 'Fifth Symphony' and 'Aztec Beauty', both deep coral-red, add splashes of colour here, too, and offer the added bonus of being unfussy about dry or wet feet and possessing semi-weeping foliage which associates well with water.

When the plantings leapt away in spring, it was hard to associate the terraces with the devastation area that had been, but the hole in the ground was still very much in evidence, filled with fetid, muddy water. I went to various water-garden specialists for advice on how to clear the murky depths, and it was here that I made the mistake which has caused me continual heartache and hard labour ever since. The advice I was given was to put into the pool generous quantities of the oxygenating weed, *Elodia canadensis*, or Canadian pondweed.

Perhaps I misunderstood, but in a very short space of time this silent invader sent out curly whorls of small leaves on branching stems to fill and choke what was quite a large expanse of water. It certainly did clear the latter, but its growth is so rampant that it constantly breaks the surface, spoiling what should be a calm, smooth expanse, and preventing reflection, which is one of the essential components of a water garden.

I have spent many weary hours, immersed to my waist, dragging out barrowload after barrowload of this wretched invader, but it remains a perennial problem. It has brought the learning of a very hard lesson, and if I may pass a piece of advice to other gardeners, it is to be very, very careful what you put into water.

We had one more project to complete. The walkway of both the right and left sides of the pool converged at the rear of the willow, over the creek which fed the pool. We had to build a bridge to span it. I envisaged an elaborate arching oriental framework; Brian said he had a much more utilitarian structure in mind!

Since we were well into winter by this time, he built the bridge in the garage. It was fascinating watching it grow, and its construction says much for his ingenuity, since he had had limited opportunity for tackling carpentry, which he enjoyed, during our nomadic years. He used a Skilsaw to cut the curved side struts of the base of the bridge, and laid two-and-three-quarter battens across them to walk on. The same battens, crossed, formed ornamental sides which he spanned with handrails.

Painted Chinese-lacquer red, the bridge looked splendid standing in the garage, and the exciting day came when it was ready to 'carry south', down the long drive to the water gardens. We had laughed and joked about making this journey, but with frequent 'put-down-the-bridge-and-rest' stops, all went well until we reached the *corner* where one turned off the drive, to step down onto the walkway around the pond. . . . We had to admit to having had a 'She'll-be-right-on-the-day' attitude to this impediment. In the event, the corner has never been quite as sharp since, we did not quite demolish the first section of the terrace, the bridge did need a certain amount of repainting and we celebrated its installation by sharing a box of bandaids between us.

CHAPTER EIGHTEEN

LOTUS:
THE SACRED FLOWER

The Lord Buddah is often depicted sitting in his joint-wrenching position on a lotus leaf. The exquisite perfection and purity of the flowers of the lotus, *Nelumbo*, rising above huge silvery leaves, have inspired poets and artists down the ages to paeans of praise. The plant is sacred to many peoples of the Buddhist religion. The Chinese regard the lotus flower as the symbol of purity because its roots often grow in filthy water and mud, but the bloom rises high above, unsullied by the corruption below.

The exotic flowers of pink, cream or yellow are borne on top of hairy stalks which may rise some 1.5 metres above the water. A separate tubular stalk supports each large round leaf, which may cover the water surface in a metre span. The underside of each leaf is deeply textured with Y-shaped veins and the reflection in the water from those which are held high is extremely beautiful.

In our subtropical area of Northland, the blooms are at their peak in sweltering February. Dragonflies of electric-blue neon hover in courtship dance on wings of gauze between the flowers' great cream petals. Late on summer evenings, the moonlight turns droplets of water on the leaf plates to pools of mercury, and jewelled frogs of emerald and gold, sitting statuesque in meditation, complete this magical ambience.

Each lotus flower is open for just three days, then the petals fall silently one by one, to float like wisps of silk across the surface of the water. When they have all fallen, a large green seedpod, like a watering-can rose, is left exposed at the top of the stalk. It is surrounded by innumerable shimmering, thread-like stamens, which are eventually also teased away by the summer breeze. The lotus flower is beautiful at all stages of its life.

The pod is a unique receptacle for the seeds, each embedded in an individual mini-womb in the flat surface of its cone shape. Once the flower petals have fallen, the stalk droops forward to allow the pod to face down towards the water so that its seeds may fall to germinate in the fertile mud of the pool.

Still bitterly regretting the invasion of the oxygenating weed *Elodia canadensis*, which I had put into the pond with my own hand, I must warn fellow gardeners at this point to heed another cautionary tale, before rushing off to procure and plant such beauty for themselves.

The lotus plant has a whitish, banana-like rootstock which multiplies by sending out stealthy fingers to root down again like strawberry suckers, thus forming new plants. Allowing this to happen by failing to confine my plants in escape-proof containers proved my undoing in the Northland climate, which is very much to its liking.

I planted in the pond two precious roots of *Nelumbo nucifera* 'Alba', which bears huge creamy flowers and bosses of long, silky, golden stamens. I planted them in large plastic open-meshed laundry baskets lined with hessian, through which the vigorous rootstocks subsequently had little trouble in escaping. In the heat of December, the plants threw up tightly furled leaves which opened into magnificent silver plates, some standing umbrella tall above the water, and some floating with tranquil drift across its surface. In January, tall stalks rose up, topped by huge buds, their outer petals folded tight in intricate precision. The heat of February opened the buds into great cream flowers of enchanting purity.

When the flowers had all gone, the large pods on their tall stalks looked so beautiful I left them, until they fell face down into the pool. It may be that many of the seeds germinated, as well as the rootstock multiplying, because I was truly amazed in the second year to find almost half the surface of the pond covered with lotus leaves.

In due course, the beauty of the massed leaves and flowers was a spectacular sight, and the inspiration for much garden photography by family and visitors. However, it was obvious that between the trailing hair of the *Elodia* and the lotus, I should soon have hardly any tranquil expanses of water left for the reflection of the sky and trees, or for glimpsing the dart of fish, which are the pleasures of water gardens.

I realised that I would have to remove a number of the plants before they completely took over the whole pond. Drastic measures followed when they died back at the end of their season in May. This involved many backbreaking, soggy hours, hands working unseen underwater, uprooting the surplus plants. It wasn't easy, because the lotus roots deeply, and the family soon became used to the wrinkled, prune-like apparition, covered in evil-smelling slime, which haunted the pond. 'I'm sure Aquarius never looked like you, Mum,' said number one daughter.

The excess plants were given to friends, with severe warnings to plant them in large containers strong and deep enough to provide imprisonment for their unruly rootstock. I planted those I wished to retain in deep barrels and heavy-duty polythene tubs offering no escape routes.

The cultivation requirements of the lotus follows those advocated for tropical waterlilies. The rootstocks should be planted horizontally about 2.5 centimetres beneath enriched soil in a large container, and submerged to a water depth of 30 centimetres. As the young foliage emerges, the containers should gradually be lowered until they are submerged to a depth of 60 centimetres. In larger pools, the plant, once established, is happy in depths of a metre or more.

In May, when all the flowers have gone and the pond is a sea of soldier-straight stalks topped by stunning seedpods, it is wise to harden one's heart and cut them off to prevent invasion by new plants through seeding. Hung upside-down and dried, they make dramatic material for floral arrangements. In late summer, I no longer have any choice about wading into the pool, cold with the first chill of autumn, to cut the magnificent lotus pods, because they have been 'discovered' by the eagle-eyed ladies of our local floral-art club.

Lord Buddha would surely have approved of the unique seed receptacles of his sacred flower finishing life in one of the artistic dried-flower creations wrought by their nimble fingers? Better still, Brian and I have the reward for the eighteen month's brutal toil it took to make the vision of oriental water gardens complete. Just two years ago we had had a fetid mud-hole in the ground which was a nightmare of erosion and vampirish insects. Now we have a clear pond to stroll around with the dogs late on summer evenings, to fall willing victims to the bewitching spell cast by the lotus flowers' great cream blossoms, gilded with the moon's silvery, shivery silence.

CHAPTER NINETEEN

THE MEDITATION GARDEN

Lotus blossoms we might have, but a rest on the proverbial laurels was shortlived! Another mega-challenge loomed. What were we to do with the rectangular area some ten by four metres which stood forlorn and unlovely at the far side of the red-lacquered bridge at the rear of the pond? The creek, rippling in during winter, kept the ground partially flooded, but when it slowed to a trickle in summer, the soil baked into spectacular clay cracks. It was a horrible mess, and just about the most inhospitable home for plant life one could imagine.

'Too far from the house for drainage or irrigation projects,' declared Brian. 'Concrete it over, and stand some pots, gnomes or whatever on it.' Such words are heard by any gardener worth her salt as the ultimate in challenges. Again, the philosophy – 'if you can't beat it, make a focal point of it'.

Into battle. The proximity of the area to the large pond and the creek trickling into it dictated an extension of the watery theme. I knew the first plantings would have to be of two small shade trees if any other plants at all were to survive the bake-out months. The search began. Gardening oracles suggested trees aplenty whose fetish was having their roots baked, but they definitely weren't into wet feet. The recommended possibilities

– alders, willows or swamp cypress – would have rapidly outgrown the small garden and required murderous pruning to keep them to size.

Head-scratching continued until I read of the willow *Salix babylonica* 'Annularis' – ram's horn willow. This curious willow has green leaves curled into neat rings ('Annularis' means ring-shaped) often encircling the branches, provides a good shade tree of neat, erect habit with airy structure and (hallelujah!) is equally at home in wet or dry soils. I planted a pair in the fertile boggy ground that autumn, and they shot away.

I watched apprehensively as the ground dried into cracks in summer when the creek ceased to run, watering them by hand, but they took the extremes in their stride. Two years on, they have grown to a height of two or three metres, upright and delicate in growth, their curly foliage much admired by visitors and, best of all, providing the small garden with much-needed shade.

Assured of their survival, the next stage was hauling yet more rocks . . . large, flat stones womanfully heaved along their journey across the paddocks with barrack-room oaths and crowbar. I needed to create a stepping-stone path through the garden for access during its underwater moods. Laying the stones to a winding pathway, it occurred to me that a small pool tucked into one curve would associate well with the willows and look cool and inviting while the garden was in drought. Even better, it would also minimise the area to find miracle plants for!

I laid a piece of rope in the shape of a pool and dug the hole to a gently sloping depth of about a metre, using the same basic method we had used for the ornamental pond on the front lawn. I lined the hole with an insulating layer of sand and lay heavy-duty black polythene as the pool liner. An equally easy method would have been to use a pre-cast fibreglass shell from the garden centre, but a few metres of polythene is just as effective and very much less expensive for so small a pool. I barrowed more attractive flat rocks to hold down, conceal and edge the polythene liner. Brian, nobly abandoning his vision of concrete and pots, helped me run a length of alkathene piping from the creek into the pool to keep it filled. During the winter months, the water spills and gurgles merrily over the edge, creating a bog-garden situation.

During the first summer, when the creek ran low, I had to top the pool up with buckets of water, but it seemed little work for the amount of pleasure it gave. (The following year, the husband, liking what he saw in the new garden, kept the pool filled by linking it to the irrigation system from the main gardens.)

Bordered by the lacquer-red bridge, with the lotus pond's great willow on the far side, the garden now had its basic foundation landscaping – two shade trees, a stepping-stone path and a small pool. Inspiration struck one morning as I sat contemplating the patterns of the sky reflected in the water – I would extend the oriental theme by creating a Chinese meditation garden beneath the willows.

For several weeks I had been heaving a particularly prized piece of kauri root (dragged up from the swamp on one of my car-abusing forays) around the garden, trying to find exactly the right spot for it. Its roots were curved and fluted like a cathedral roof, and standing balanced on end over the small pool, it looked just perfect. A visit to my (dangerously near) garden centre found a benignly smiling Buddha figure to sit meditating beneath the wooden arches of the kauri 'cathedral'.

When buying fish for the pool, I saw in the aquarium-supply section several baskets of small rounded pebbles, bleached and scoured by some great river in the South Island. I knew how marvellous they would look around the edges of the meditation pool, and having asked the price, could scarcely believe my good fortune when the assistant said, 'They've been sitting round for ages. You can have the lot for twenty dollars.' Around the small pool I tipped them out of the bags slowly, so that they fell one over the other as the river might have tumbled them, and the sun bleached their scoured smoothness to oyster white. They created the most natural of edgings.

To the left of the meditation pool, the golden willow at the rear of the large pond had grown so rapidly that it was cascading weeping tendrils above the bridge crossing the new small garden. The soft green foliage looked wonderful with the red lacquer of the woodwork, and I saw that, in time, these branches might be trained to create a cool green tunnel. This was an unforeseen combination, one of those happy accidents in the garden (like the Brides Walk) which bring so much pleasure. I placed two seats of gnarled wood beneath the trunk of the willow, and this cool green corridor to the left of the meditation garden has become one of our favourite spots in the garden, especially in summer.

The basic landscaping complete, the dreaded search began for miracle plants to clothe the inhospitable area. My first regret was that all the faithful silvery leafed, drought-loving plants were out – they would drown in winter – while bog-loving plants would shrivel up in summer. Problems? Problems? No. Challenges, challenges! Much midnight reading of gardening oracles continued until a chapter on 'marginals', those plants which will tolerate wet feet, and also survive dry periods with a little help, offered great hope.

The period of plant experimentation began, and I admit to a shamefully high incidence of plant murder during the first year, particularly among the dainty little candelabra primula (*P. heladoxa*) for which I lusted desperately, but I can now write confidently of the toughies that survived, finding bog or bake no great hassle.

Hemerocallis, the daylilies, have been a great joy, adapting to both conditions with equal ease, and always so generous with their flowers. I would recommend them for any difficult area of the garden. *Hemerocallis* 'Amazing Grace', with a rich ivory-cream trumpet flower and apple-green heart, associated beautifully with cream-and-green-foliaged hostas, *H.* 'Francee' and *H.* 'Ginkgo Craig'. The hostas thrived during the damp months, and survived with minimal watering during the dry months as the foliage of the taller *Hemerocallis* and the willows gave them shade.

The native flax, *Phormium* 'Yellow Wave', with attractive green-and-yellow-striped, weeping foliage, took all extremes of ground conditions in its stride. *Phormium* 'Maori Maiden', also of weeping form, provided a warm splash of sunset reds, together with *Lobelia cardinalis* 'Queen Victoria', which has tapering spikes of vivid deep scarlet flowers and red foliage. The silver-sword leaves of the bold native *Astelia chathamica* made a stunning foil for the reds and provided a note of drama against the weeping foliage of the other flaxes.

For taller plantings, *Zantedeschia* 'Green Goddess', with cream-and-green-washed flowers and luxuriant foliage, gave a stately effect. Clumps of the dwarf *Zantedeschia* 'Little Gem' and *Z.* 'Little Child', which flower from spring through summer, are attractive planted in small pockets. I love to look at their flattish blooms, pale and mysterious in the moonlight.

As each new plant established itself and survived the seasonal conditions least appreciated, groundcover was formed, helping the earth to conserve moisture and dry out less in high summer. Each plant that came through both extremes was a victory. The cream-and-green variegated form of the common figwort, *Scrophularia aquatica*, has proved to be a winner. It retains its attractive ruffled foliage all summer and bears spires of small maroon flowers. It is easily propagated from cuttings, lightens darker corners and, like the hostas, tolerates the drier months with minimal watering.

No meditation garden would have been complete without a generous proportion of the noble iris. Those which have survived well are *Iris kaempferi*, the Japanese iris, whose horizontal petals looking like large butterflies, *I. laevigata*, predominantly blue-coloured with golden yellow markings, and varieties of *I. sibirica*, which have been remarkably good-natured about whether their feet were wet or dry.

I enjoyed filling odd corners with *I. sisyrinchium*, the dwarf satin iris, a delightful small plant with fine iris-like leaves and flowers of blue, white and yellow. The species grows to a height of about twenty centimetres and is tolerant of almost all soils and situations.

As background planting to the garden, complementary to the oriental theme, I planted a pot of the pretty arching fairy bamboo, *Bambusa gracilis*. Remembering only too well the weeks of hard labour it took Brian and I to chainsaw, haul away and burn the wall of bamboo devouring the drive, I sunk the plant in a strong container to be sure of restricting its growth to suit the small garden.

It was fun to put life into the small pool with the pair of goggle-eyed Black Moor fish, with wavy fan-like tails. A pair of orange Chinese Celestials, with huge protruding, upward-poised eyes, made a delightful contrast to the Black Moors. Given the sheltering pads of the white miniature waterlily, *Nymphaea pygmaea* 'Alba', to swim beneath, they thrive, and I am sure Lord Buddha's smile is even more benign as he contemplates the tranquil scene. He is kept company by a Chinese figurine of an old fisherman, whose line trails gently among the fish he will never catch.

Recently, as a luxurious finishing touch to the Chinese garden I have allowed myself three dwarf trees in oriental lacquered pots – *Acer* 'Chisio' and *A.* 'Katsura', both especially lovely in spring and autumn, are ideal container subjects. The tree in the third pot is *Robinia* 'Mop Top', delightful in an oriental garden, with curly leaves in summer and contorted bare branches giving much interest in winter. It is possible to have these small treasures now, because the developing willows afford their delicate foliage the shade and shelter they need. A generous cupful of 'Liquid Rain' crystals mixed in the potting mix at the time of planting the trees in their containers keeps watering to a minimum in all but the hottest weather. Their dwarf form and the delicate tracery of their foliage is a perfect foil to the plants that are the 'toughies' – the hardy survivors.

Suddenly my meditation garden was beginning to look established, but (like all the best gardens) it is not yet finished, because in the two years since its creation I have continued, with much interest, to experiment with other plants which will, in this difficult bog-to-bake situation, survive – and even thrive!

GARDENS OF CHILDHOOD

Shortly after we had completed the meditation garden, our daughter Sarah came home on holiday, evoking memories of a different sort. She is a cool and trendy student. She is at the stage of saving the world single-handed, and the thought of making us grandparents is light years away in her scheme of things.

While home, she took six sunflower seeds from the cockatiel's dish, and potted them up in the greenhouse. She fussed and fretted over their germination and troubled infancy (too much water), then transplanted them with immense care into my vege garden. The dynamic young feminist said, 'Mum, do you remember the sunflower seeds I used to grow in my own garden when I was little, and how you used to measure their height against mine as they grew, and all those doll's mud-pie tea-parties we used to have?'

I had not forgotten and, sitting that day in my present garden in an autumn that was a gift of blue and gold, we talked of the gardens of our respective childhoods. We crossed a span of some three decades, leading us down the years now called, 'Do you remember?'

We tiptoed back into gardens that had been our very own

private places, a quiet plot that was ours to dig and cultivate, where adults were welcome only by invitation; childrens' gardens planted in scattered disorder where radishes were planted in circles around a centrepiece of a huge cauliflower; where pansies played among the cabbages, and nasturtiums romped up giant sunflowers which were our pride and joy.

Do you remember those gardens of childhood which looked like minefields because we had been digging for treasure? The soil yielded loot much loved by small brothers – old nails, bits of wire, metal bottle tops and marbles. We excavated priceless fragments of prettily painted china and pottery, pieces of coloured glass, bits of old clay pipes, shards of mirror, buttons, old tins and, best of all, *real* treasure in the form of an old coin. All guarded and hoarded jealously, swapped only for a piece one coveted more, from the collection of a playmate or sibling.

Do you remember the enthusiastic waterings of feet and rows we'd planted, that changed from strange seeds into flowers? And those that didn't when temptation proved too strong, and we peeped beneath the soil . . . coveted plants of bold bright colours sneaked from adults' gardens which did not survive their rootless transplantation to gardens of our own . . . buds we 'helped' open, and tiny shoots we 'aided' through the earth?

Can you recall childish fantasies given by the colours and scents of the flowers of childhood? Fingers tipped with foxglove flowers, 'foxy fingers' or 'fairy gloves' because the fairies lived in the flowers' freckled bells; of searching desperately for these elusive creatures that 'lived at the bottom of the garden'; of the dainty plates of our best flowers we left there to tempt them to reveal themselves?

We pinched antirrhinum flowers to make funny faces, or snarl as fearsome dragons' jaws. We sat dolls stiffly to attention at tea parties around plates of fried eggs – limnanthes flowers – and luscious cakes and pies of mud decorated with brilliant blooms. We rubbed the furry silver leaves of *Stachys lanata*, lambs' ears, against our cheeks, and made 'granny's bonnet' hats for tiny dolls from *Aquilegia* flowers, which were winged like a dove and spurred like an eagle.

We cheated in our blowing of dandelion clocks, we blew softly, so softly, in delicious terror of the old adage, 'Child, take a dandelion clock and blow upon it three times. If all the seeds blow away, 'tis a sign your mother doesn't want you. If some of the seeds remain, then she does.'

Do you remember when the confines of the garden hedges, walls and fences was our world of play and make-believe, a world peopled by cowboys and Indians, cops and robbers, and secret gangs? When the pond became the high seas plagues by pirates we fought with fearsome homemade swords, and the lawns made threadbare in summer from our games of cricket, rounders and football?

Do you remember shrubberies which existed only for us to build lovingly constructed dens and hideouts; when the trees held us and our treehouses in their arms, and listened to our secrets? We hid in these small, green worlds, lost to prying adult eyes, where their voices calling for bedtime could be heard, but ignored because we could not 'hear' them. How safe we felt in the green confines of these shadowy small worlds, stockaded by flowers and leaves, hideouts where the sun filtered through in dappled gold.

We looked down on our gardens from these secret places and planned the destiny of our plants, loving the weeds that were our finest crops, bestowing them in hot-handed admiring bunches on favourite adults. We stood on tiptoe and stretched up small eager hands when they let us pick 'real' flowers like roses and lilies, remembering to do as we were told, and pick 'nice long stems, not just the heads . . .'.

Do you remember, as Sarah does, measuring your small

height against hollyhocks, delphiniums and sunflowers which seemed to reach forever into the sky above? Hours spent making necklaces of daisy chains, and coronets of gold from marigolds, when our identities were those of princes and princesses? Of gathering baskets of blossom from fruit trees in spring to shower over brides when we were playing 'weddings'? Of bursting with pride when the tomatoes, radish or lettuce on the adults' plates were from *our* gardens (and the potatoes weren't, because we'd dug ours up to count how many were underneath, or see if they'd grown bigger since yesterday)?

Do you remember the state funerals in the garden accorded to dead birds, pet mice, hamsters, and beloved cats and dogs? Reaching back down the years, my daughter and I could both feel again the terrible but transient anguish of childhood over small graves marked with wooden crosses of our own making. We remembered the heartbroken, bawling sorrow which accompanied the writing of names such as 'Joey', 'Bess', and 'Pussy Willow' in rounded childish script on homemade crosses. They were decked with huge bunches of flowers hitherto forbidden, because for reasons we didn't then fully understand, these were times when the adults cried too.

We lay among plants where insects crawled, unaware of our curious fascination. We studied, then trapped them, put them in jam-jar prisons and tins, and did awful things to them . . . had pet ladybirds and black beetles which lived (sometimes) in grubby matchboxes in our pockets. We held snail, slug, and worm races, and frog 'jumps' in secret places in the garden, because it was sport forbidden by adults, bringing swift and certain punishment if we were found out. We pitted our champions one against the other, with the uncomprehending cruelty of childhood.

Do you remember the revolting little brothers who hid in the garden with their friends, and jumped out to drop a worm down the neck of a sister's frock, or opened a hand containing a huge hairy spider or unhappy toad in front of her face?

Do you remember climbing trees and searching shrubs for birds' bests, and lying awake with the terrible companion of your conscience, because you had stolen a poor bird's eggs; or worse, of knowing that those fledglings lying cold and dead in the nest were lifeless because you had 'played' with them; of understanding, even then, that all the blankets of leaves and grass in the world wouldn't make them warm and all gapey-mouthed again? The depths of that childish guilt, that education by beauty and by fear, this we could remember as though it were only yesterday.

We felt no such guilt in robbing the trees of their tiny hard fruit, before autumn had come to plump and ripen them. We danced beneath the apple trees in the orchard, chanting:

> *Apple tree, apple tree,*
> *Bear apples for me;*
> *Hats full, caps full,*
> *Sacks full, laps full*
> *Apple tree, apple tree,*
> *Bear apples for me!*

I remember only too well howling with that peculiar bellyache which comes from eating unripe fruit . . .

There were days in the garden when all that was happening was summer, which seemed to go on forever. Exhausted from rampaging games, we threw ourselves down in grass which was almost as tall as we were. We lay on our backs, sucking the honeyed ears of clover flowers and the sun-sweetened sap of grass stalks. We watched crawling insects and butterflies staring up in the blue bowl of the sky until, dizzied by the clouds' floating, we fell asleep with summer.

Sometimes we would beg to be allowed to camp out on the

lawn on hot summer nights. Our play tent was an old blanket draped over a let-down washing line, weighted at the sides with stones. We would tell ghost stories, clutching each other in delicious terror, and somehow, we were always woken up in our own beds in the house by a smiling adult, the morning after our camp-out nights.

Sarah recalled golden hours spent making elaborate miniature gardens in old bowls, baking dishes or trays, decorating them splendidly with flowers of the brightest and the best; of creating for them mirror lakes, trees of twigs, paths of sand or tiny pebbles, the houses made of matchboxes with doors and windows drawn in.

'If I have children, they must have gardens, Mum,' she said.

We remembered days of lost and happy hours spent distilling 'medicines' and wonderful perfumes in old cough-mixture bottles. I remember the chagrin of getting smacked for drinking some of the 'medicines' when I got bored with trying to force them past my dolls' unyielding lips, and the delight when Mum said she would 'wear the whole bottle' of my rose-petal and violet perfume when she went out later.

Do you remember autumns when you helped adults collect garden refuse (without being bribed) for the joy of building bonfires; of dancing wildly and dangerously near the crackling frames, shrieking like banshees, with streaming eyes, smoky hair; of coughing and spluttering, and burning your hands and mouth on potatoes half-cooked from the fire?

Do you remember winters when the garden was the best playground ever, because it was suddenly full of snow that reached to your knees? When the snowmen we built were the best in the world; when we spent the whole afternoon making 'ammo' – until our fingers froze – fat white snowballs to hurl at Dad from a shrubbery ambush when he came home from work?

I remember Sarah's great-grandmother telling my brother and I to look at the snow 'falling as thick as a burst-open feather pillow'. It is almost as though those feathery flakes have drifted down more than half a century, to become the dim and quiet memories for which her great-grand-daughter and I were together reaching. Memories as silent as snowflakes, of the gardens of childhood which had settled in our hearts and now whispered to us from years long gone.

In those to come, when all my young student's causes are fought and won, if she should bring into our lives the gift of grandchildren, how much I wish, how very much I wish them gardens of their own, so that one day they will say to my daughter, 'Yes. Yes. I *remember . . .*'

As for rosemary
I let it run all over my garden walls,
Not only because the bees love it,
But because 'tis the herb
Sacred to remembrance.

Sir Thomas More

CHAPTER TWENTY-ONE

GORSE, RAGWORT AND HEARTBREAK CLAY

The homestead is approached by a long, steep drive some two hundred metres in length, which had been bulldozed through the paddocks to facilitate the transportation of the house to the site on the top of the hill. The drive had been tarsealed by previous owners, for which we are ever grateful, but it had been cut at a lower level than the paddocks so that a shallow gorge had been created.

Both sides of the gorge had worn into eroded banks of clay, and in the rough debris at their feet, swathes of noxious weeds cavorted, self-sowing themselves with extreme generosity. It occurred to me that the fact that the homestead luxuriated in cottage and Elizabethan gardens at the back and a gorse, ragwort and thistle sanctuary at the front was somewhat incongruous. The horticultural miracle pending, therefore, was the taming and planting of the drive. Observation had shown me that here lay some of the most unforgiving, heartbreak clay on the property.

Pliny the Elder, the Roman naturalist (AD 33–79), wrote, 'The earth, gentle and indulgent, ever subservient to the wants of man, spreads his walks with flowers, and his table with plenty; returns with interest, every good committed to her care.' I brooded on these beautiful and noble words with guilty irreverence. With the soul of a Philistine, I concluded that in Pliny's part of the Empire, the soil was composed of good, dark, rich, friable humus, not the sour prehensile orange clay with which I had fought a one-woman battle for the last four years. It is strong, tenacious stuff; it clings magnificently to boots, spades, the wheel of the barrow, gloves, socks and the knees of slacks, so that the garden is gradually transferred to the toolshed, the garage, doorsteps, patios, verandas and eventually the bedroom, from where it is despatched to the laundry.

In my days as a novice gardener, I hacked and chiselled holes for shrubs and trees that were bursting with rude good health in their planter bags. The holes became caverns with sides like concrete, which proved impermeable to plants with the most rampageous of roots. I filled them with the delicious organic mixtures recommended by gardening oracles, put in the plants, and watered them with missionary zeal.

I watered daily; plants began to wilt. I watered more; they dropped their leaves. It occurred to me that they were not at all well. Fearing the worst, I remember pulling up, with much squelching and gurgling, a rhododendron. I had not been aware of rhododendrons' aversion to sodden clay. Its roots were quite rotten. I pulled up a few more shrubs; the compost and organic matter with which I'd packed the holes floated to the surface of the water which now filled them. Claypan coffins.

These were the days before Harold had taught me how to dig extra big holes with drainage materials at their base. But for him, I should probably still be tenderly dropping plants into mini swimming pools, a kind of horticultural burial at sea.

I took to reading books on the structure of soil (excellent material for the insomniac) and learned that clay is composed of very minute particles packed densely together so that porosity is minimised. It appeared that it is this lack of soil structure and porosity which is the kiss of death to the roots of plants which require as much oxygen as their leaves.

Learned tomes instructed on the assessment of one's soil — if it is black or very dark brown, this is a good sign, if yellowish orange, pale brown, or streaky grey and mottled — not so good. Dark soil is rich in organic material so it will be easier to work and the plants will thrive. If, on picking up a lump of your soil and rubbing it between your fingers, it feels cold and a bit like plasticine, and sticks together in a clammy lump, guess what? Real estate agents should be compelled by law to provide the prospective buyer of every property they sell with a complete soil analysis report.

Karel Capek, writing in his *Gardeners' Year* (1929), likens good soil to good food. He says that if you can lift a full spade easily,

> *it gives you a feeling as appetising and gratifying as if you lifted food with a full ladle, and with a full spoon. A good soil, like good food, must not be either too fat, or heavy, or cold, or wet, or dry, or greasy, or hard, or gritty, or raw; it ought to be like bread, like gingerbread, like a cake, like leavened dough. It should crumble, but not break into lumps; under the spade it ought to crack but not squelch; it must not make slabs, or blocks, or honeycombs, or dumplings; but, when you turn it over with a spade, it ought to breathe with pleasure and fall into a fine and puffy tilth. That is tasty and edible soil, cultured and noble, deep and moist, permeable, breathing and soft . . .*

I fantasise about soil like this; soil which receives the thrust of a spade, welcomes it even; soil that allows itself to be turned over without sending jarring thrusts of RSI through the wrists, elbows and shoulders; soil that does not repel one's tools or try, squelching rudely, to grab and cling to them forever.

If you have soil that is workable, volcanic even, imagine if by some dreadful chance, you had to move from the plot on which you spend every 'leisure' moment slaving, and inherit an acre of clay — clay that is cold, wet and unyielding; clay that requires explosives to crack it apart for the insertion of conditioning materials; clay like lead, primeval weeping clay which oozes ill temper and turns itself in wet weather into an unworkable sticky putty, greasy mass, heavy like lead. Attempt to work it, and every spadeful you lift makes you buckle at the knees.

In summer this clay bakes hard enough to open into chasms which any self-respecting earthquake would have been proud to inflict. You can try to smash it with a pickaxe, ram it with a crowbar, savage its chunks with a mallet, while you roar barrack-room oaths and loud lamentations. In hot weather clay becomes bricks, in cold weather, icecream bricks. In warmer weather, clay compacts admirably under foot traffic and has the reputation of making fine tennis courts, cricket pitches or areas where good ball bounce is required. For beds compacted thus in the garden, it is better to forget your spade and hire a pneumatic drill, or dabble in illegal explosives.

Lawns laid on clay are something else again; they remain wet and soggy in all but the driest weather. They are beloved of children and dogs, since they lend themselves admirably to skids and slides of epic proportions. But there is help at hand: you can dig a network of cutoff drains, open to the surface, across, beside or beneath the lawn. I am uncertain about the effect this paddy-field irrigation network might have on the aesthetic aspect of the lawns. I fret that children, guests, dogs, lawnmowers, tools, etc, might disappear into their watery depths forever.

On the other hand, if such drainage channels are dug to ring the entire gardens, a novel moat and portcullis effect could be achieved, or they might serve as a gigantic water-filled ha-ha. The author of this particular advice omits to mention that it would probably kill you, or take decades, to gouge such channels from the clay. He does, in all fairness, suggest alternatives, which are:

1. Avoid all foot traffic in the area.
2. Cover the entire area with planks or duckboards.

Perhaps the children and dogs could use these as diving boards from which to leap into the depths of the uncovered drainage channels. They smack of fractured femurs for older gardeners.

Regarding the size of planting holes in clay soils (a subject on which I have become remarkably touchy), he waxes most enthusiastic. One must get out the post-hole borer, or digger, and excavate holes at least two metres wide and deep for shrubs and trees. The bases must be lined with copious quantities of rock, which needs to be hewn from a quarry, or delivered at excessive cost, or with anything else which is prohibitively heavy but will constitute drainage material. If you live on an average-to-small suburban section, this will ease your planting problems, since you will only have room for five plants. As to having post-hole borers and diggers immediately to hand, I should forget it and stick to pots.

If, like me, you are pigheaded, have nothing better to do and must persist in combat, there are *ways* to break up and improve the enemy. Without exception, they entail abusing the body with a horrendous amount of hard labour. This is the only way in which the pan may be broken, for the insertion of the thousand barrowloads of the lime, coarse sand, peat, shingle, metal, rocks, organic materials, possums or anything at all you can think of to make it *better*.

CHAPTER TWENTY-TWO

GARDENING
ON THE ROCKS

The morning I wheeled my weapons down the drive to begin warfare, I concluded that the name of the game was going to be *survival*; a kind of natural selection, where only the toughest of plant species would survive. But before any planting could be done, the erosion of the slopes had to be tackled. We needed no contractors for this. We had served our apprenticeship stabilising the banks around the water gardens and were experts. It was back to barrowing, roping, heaving and crowbarring rocks from the paddocks.

We piled up these rocks and dug them in, making a backward-sloping rockery wall to seal the banks. Wherever there was a chink, nook or cranny in the concrete clay, I rammed in compost between the rocks and marked it as a planting pocket.

The drive rockeries were not built in a day, or in a year. I began to think dynasties would rise and fall before we ever finished them. Although the lower areas had been begun by the previous owner, there were still, counting both sides, slopes some three hundred metres in length (2.5 metres in height in some places) to cover and stabilise. The rockeries were built (painfully) over a period of two years, in whatever time we could spare from the farm, business and the rest of the garden.

Planting was slow because stabilisation took priority and because every plant had to go in with pickaxe and crowbar. A plant only qualified if it had 'hardy' printed in black and white on its planter label. After four years of breaking clay, and watching it turn from bog-to-bake and back again, I had learned to be wary of any species that were labelled 'easy care', and of those which garden-centre staff swore would 'look after themselves'.

In addition to the Three Great Truths which had been revealed to me while creating the tree lawns, I had grasped a Fourth Great Truth as my gardening experience matured; an 'easy care' plant will only thrive, just like any other, if the environment and planting situation in which it is put are correct. In other words, I had perceived that the condition of the soil correlates quite closely with the survival or demise of the plant. I regret to say that an enormous amount of plant murder has led me to this secret of good horticulture.

The plants still had to be committed to the ground with brute force, but things were far from doom and gloom. As I began planting the dread drive, I made the happiest of discoveries. Although the soil beneath the organic goodies with which I packed the holes was still swinish clay, the holes did not fill and become waterlogged, because they were on slopes. Surface water drained naturally down through the rocks leaving, contrary to my wildest expectations, conditions that were generally hot and dry. It was my Grand Discovery, my great bonus. It was as though a whole new world of gardening had suddenly opened up to me. For the first time ever, I could incorporate drought-resistant plants into the grand scheme. The numbers of plants which worship the sun and revel in arid conditions far exceeds those which like to paddle.

Along the drive I could have lashings of plants with silver foliage, which the gardening gurus insist we must have to tone down warmer colours, and those which are so vulgar they leap out and smite one between the eyes – orange tiger-lilies, wicked acid-yellow marigolds and their ilk. I lost little time in planting all the *Artemisia* varieties, *A. arborescens* being particularly useful, since it forms a good spreading shrub of immensely attractive fine-cut silver foliage. The toughie *Senecio greyii*, with downy foliage, also fulfils this criterion, and for silvery groundcover, *Helichrysum argyrophyllum* roots as it spreads, finding footholds between the stones.

I could now plant all manner of sun-loving daises, the chrysanthemum and marguerite species, gazanias, arctotis and coreopsis. A hardy shrub daisy which never stops flowering is *Euryops pectinatus*. In addition to yellow flowers, it has silvery grey foliage and would, I think, survive anywhere. The Cape daisy, *Dimorphotheca*, forms a thick mat of attractive foliage smothered with gay, daisy-like flowers of white, pinks, wine, purple-mauves or creamy yellow. There is an excellent hybrid named 'Silver Sparkle', with cream-and-green-variegated foliage, and one called 'Catherine Wheel', rejoicing in flower petals which are pinched at their tips like tiny spoons.

Now I could experiment with species such as *Mesembryanthemum* or ice plants. The disparity in the nomenclature of this species eludes me, since the plant is practically a succulent and would probably form a groundcover in the Sahara. I also planted the merry little nasturtium 'Whirly Bird', but not too near the ice plants, since both are considered to fall into the less than tasteful colour spectrum. Both looked very well cooled by the dark blue chalice flowers of the groundcovering *Convolvulus mauritanicus*, and with the white blooms and silver foliage of *C. cneorum*.

On the flower front, no self-respecting clay bank would be seen dead without generous quantities of *Agapanthus*. The survival ratings of this plant are legendary. In addition to the true blue, there are now a number of excellent hybrids with an extended colour range of violets, mauve-pink and white. A dwarf variety with delightful variegated foliage of cream and green named 'Tinkerbell' is also available.

The great globose seedheads of the *Agapanthus* are attractive all winter, especially when candied with frost. I cannot see this plant without thinking of the story I was told about a gardener who, tired of people using her open-plan lawn as a short cut, put up the notice 'Beware of the Agapanthus'. This apparently worked like charm, but I do not swear to the veracity of the tale.

Among the smaller shrubs enhancing the hot dry banks, the *Cistus* ('rock rose') varieties with their flamboyant and prolific flowers have become well loved. *C. corbariensis* is one of the hardiest species, giving yellow-centred white flowers above grey-green aromatic foliage. *C. ladaniferus* has large white flowers with a fascinating eye of maroon dotted black, *C.* 'Silver Pink' is one of the prettiest hybrids, giving dark pink flowers bedecked with gold stamens. *C.* 'Bennet's White' is perhaps the aristocrat of the species. Although not as generous with her blooms as the others, they are magnificent – large white silky flowers with an enormous boss of golden stamens, which resemble those of a white rose or those of the temperamental white tree poppy, *Romneya coulteri*.

The cooling blue flowers of the shrubs *Plumbago* and *Ceanothus* (Californian lilac) are enjoyed in this area where the sun beats up from the tarseal. There are many hybrids of the latter shrub, but I consider *C. papillosus roweanus* one of the most versatile blue-flowering shrubs grown. Its heads of deep-blue blooms almost hide its miniature rich green foliage and appear over a long period.

Many of the excellent natives I had used on the hot dry terrace above the water gardens adapted well to life on the rockeries. With generous helpings of 'Liquid Rain' in their planting compost, and feet beneath the rocks, they thrive, giving year-round colour. The phormiums, cordylines, coprosmas,

Pseudopanax, *Pittosporum*, *Leucospermum* and native grasses give a wide variety of foliage form, shape and colour. For rich red and mahogany tones, I interplanted the natives with *Photinia* 'Red Robin' and *Berberis thunbergii* 'Atropurpurea'. Although the latter is deciduous, it never seems to be so for very long in Northland, and has the added bonus of giving brilliant autumnal scarlets, oranges and golds.

Blue-toned hebes looked attractive illuminated by cream and green variegated flaxes such as *P.* 'Yellow Wave', and *P. cookianum* 'Tricolor'. *Hebe* 'Wiri Dawn' is an outstanding prostrate variety of weeping form with rose-pink buds, excellent for spilling over banks and rocks. *Hebe* 'Icing Sugar', with blooms tipped pink and white, like apple blossom, makes an excellent companion plant for shrubs with silver or dark-red foliage.

I had one bonus on my journey along the hot and rocky road, and that was one area of dappled shade and cool. Just before the left bank of the water gardens, the drive was shadowed on either side by the totaras in the paddocks. It seemed a natural progression to link these areas with repeated similar plantings. Because the clay here was damp but not sodden, I was able to put in ponga underplanted with hydrangeas and the native *Arthropodium cirrhatum* (rengarenga or rock lily). The parasols of ponga have created a cool oasis in an otherwise very hot area.

Since I was planting over such a wide area, and on two sides, I found it was important to judiciously repeat groups of plantings, to avoided a spotty, isolated effect. This also gave a sense of unity and much more visual impact to the area as a whole. Clumps of the ever-versatile *Hemerocallis* (daylily), were excellent for repeated plantings.

The drive was not wide enough to allow for many shade trees, but several groups of *Cedrela sinensis*, the Chinese toon, have been a joy. When we arrived in Northland in the spring of 1987, I saw the flamboyant shrimp-pink foliage of this handsome tree everywhere and was intrigued by it. The name of the tree is derived from *Cedrus*, because its wood is similar in appearance and fragrance to some of the cedar species. The tree bears straight and erect branches on which the striking new rosy foliage ages to cream, and then to green. The tree grows to approximately four by three metres and is perfectly suited to hot, dry conditions. Its only disadvantage is that it is loved by possums.

My other tree planting, in an inlet between paddock gates, was of a group of the silver birch, *Betula pendula* 'Tristis'. Although the tree is tall growing, its light and airy structure did not overwhelm the narrow drive. This species is much more tolerant of inhospitable planting conditions than is generally realised. Though attractive at all times of the year, I enjoy it most in autumn, when its delicate pendulous branches appear to be laden with cascades of gold coins, coffers to make King Midas himself hyperventilate! When such deciduous trees let fall their leaves, winter colour may be achieved at their feet with plantings of bulbs. Those which will tolerate dry conditions include *Allium*, *Amaryllis*, *Babiana*, *Ixia*, *Nerine*, *Romulea* and *Sparaxis*.

Excellent providers of year-round gold and silver tones are *Cupressus* 'Golden Halo' and *Juniperus procumbens* 'Nana'. The former will eventually form a dense, low-growing groundcover of long, sweeping branches, some five to six metres wide, and the latter will cascade down over the banks in a silvery blue waterfall.

It has even been possible to incorporate a cottage-garden effect into the plantings at the top of the drive borders, where they merge with the domestic gardens. I had had a bad time in the water-retentive clay with lavenders and rosemary, the essential companions of old roses. Many went to a hasty and watery grave, but among the hot rocks they thrive.

There is still room for more plantings on the drive rockeries, which gives the stimulation of experimenting with new varieties for 'survival gardens'. My present passion is for the excellent Rugosa roses of ancient lineage and hardy nature. The fragile, crumpled tissue-paper appearance of their blooms belies their hardy nature. They are survivors par excellence, even in coastal conditions, and in Europe they are used for hedging and for block plantings along the sides of polluted motorways.

Libraries have whole sections of books on plantings for hot dry places. Got a hot, dry, clay bank to plant? Gardening on the rocks? Go for it!

CHAPTER TWENTY-THREE

THE HAPPY
WANDERERS

The happiest accidents in our gardens are often brought about by self-sowing plants. It fascinates me that no matter where they pop up, almost always in the last position one would have thought of planting them, they invariably look so right. It is true that some like *Impatiens* and forget-me-nots can be hair-tearingly invasive, but so many are welcome invaders. Every gardener has a welcome or forbidden list of 'happy wanderers' which come and go, each to their season.

One of my favourite self-sowing garden 'slaves' is *Geranium maderense*, which blooms in early spring, unlike other heat-loving members of its family which come with the summer. *G. maderense* grows to about a metre high and wide and has deeply cut handsome foliage on long reddish stalks. It smothers itself in October in a profusion of single lavender-pink flowers which last for several months. Although *G. maderense* dies back after flowering, numerous self-sown seedlings spring up quickly and soon replace the parent plant. *G. anemonifolium* is similar, but has more reddish purple flowers, equally attractive foliage and does not die back after flowering.

Cynoglossum nervosum gives sterling service almost all the year round in milder areas. The plant grows from a clump of pointed leaves to about 40 centimetres tall and bears several spires of long-lasting forget-me-not-like flowers. Seeding readily in all situations, the flowers of pinks, intense delphinium blues and whites hybridise freely, producing lovely pastel shades. They make superb underplanting for roses, giving a pink and blue cottage-garden ambience. Their only fault (which must be spoken) is that their small round seedheads are covered in tightly clinging hooks. Beware of getting them in your hair while stooping to weed — the resulting experience with a hairbrush is very painful.

An old-fashioned favourite with many gardeners is the 'poached egg plant', *Limnanthes douglasii*. I love to plant vast patches beneath early-blooming white iris, and near the variegated gold foliage of *Euonymus* 'Emeralds 'n' Gold'. The small white flowers with their golden hearts are set among delicate, lacy foliage and soon become a carpet for the bees.

Of the faithful self-sowing *Oenothera* species or evening primroses, my favourite is *O. speciosa* 'Pink Petticoat'. This plant blooms from spring until late summer, its massed, fragile-looking flowers, veined with darker pink, belying its hardy nature. It does not mind poor soil or hot, dry places. Planted in rich soil, it tends to bolt, and bloom less. One would not quarrel with these arrangements.

An equally hardy and generous lady with her seeds is *Physostegia virginiana*, the 'obedient plant', so called because of the way its hinged flower stalks will stay put when moved, and because it will grow virtually anywhere. *P. v.* 'Vivid' has deep pink tubular flowers, and 'Summer Spire' has taller heads of lilac-purple. Both bloom in massed spires from late summer to late autumn, making an excellent show when everything else in the garden is looking tired and middle-aged. Such attributes!

Two of the best escapees from the herb garden are borage, *Borago officinalis*, and golden feverfew, *Chrysanthemum parthenium aureum*. The furry-textured grey-green leaves of borage are cucumber-flavoured and delicious in salads. I like to persuade the bees to let me pick its star-shaped, gentian-blue flowers for the decoration of summer dishes, and to drop into ice-cube trays. Borage, with its cool blue-grey colourings, makes an attractive visitor to most cottage-garden borders. Golden feverfew, with dainty white daisy flowers, seems to look right no matter where it chooses to set down, but appears best of all when it chooses for its lime-gold leaves a companion plant of blue.

Perhaps the most precious of all the plants which self-sow so generously are those that plan winter colour for our gardens – *Cineraria*, with its vivid daisy heads, delicate little *Linaria* 'Fairy Bouquet', dainty multi-headed *Primula malacoides*, lemon primroses, fluffy calendulas and old favourites, the hardy small cyclamens which have attractive mottled foliage and many pink butterfly flowers giving way to exploding corkscrew seed-capsules.

It would be impossible to forget the enchanting faces of pansies and violas, especially the little 'Johnny Jump Up' varieties which can soon make an enchanting groundcover. We all have our list of favourite self-sowing plants which, in colonising, produce chance plant associations or the happy accidents which contribute so much to the overall natural tapestry of a garden. Perhaps we should take a rest more often from buying seed, trays and raising mix, sowing, pricking out and planting seedlings – give ourselves less work by letting these 'happy wanderers' roam.

> *The best gardens are something of a muddle. They have an air of happy accident, they look a little careless, however carefully in fact the whole has been planned. Things have grown up and flourished cheek by jowl, like a large family of children, some natural, some adopted, some short and some tall, some further advanced for their age than others. . . . and they tumble about together then fall into each other's arms, or else squabble perpetually until they are separated in just such a way.*
>
> Susan Hill

CHAPTER TWENTY-FOUR

WHITE QUEEN TO BLACK KNIGHT

Each time I walk past the white section of the Elizabethan Garden, the thought is there, nagging away at my brain, so that in my mind's eye I plant this garden again and again. Shall the flowers of the pale and silvery White Queen be vanquished by those of the dark and broody Black Knight? Shall he reign in a garden in its planting as black as his dusky, smouldering heart?

His plants would wear the sumptuous red-black damasks, velvets and brocades of Elizabethan princesses and their courtiers, and tell of fire from rubies in a cardinal's ring. Their foliage would be rouged and blushing with darkest garnet reds, colours from a jeweller's secret horde, and with wine colours from the cobwebby cellars of connoisseurs – clarets, burgundies, ports, roses and liquid reds as dark as bulls' blood.

It has to happen, this rebellion and act of defiance by the Black Knight against the White Queen and her appealing but hopelessly overplanted white garden. Was Major Lawrence Johnston, at the start of the twentieth century, the original Black Knight? It was he who almost committed heresy among the gardening gurus of his time, such as Jekyll and Fish, by scorning their pale pastels, and planting instead borders of bronze and copper, grape-dark reds and plum-black purples in his gardens at Hidcote Manor in Gloucestershire.

Our Black Knight, having seized the White Queen's lands, and sent her to an ivory tower to languish in a proper (but not too uncomfortable) manner, would choose an area of full light to create his moody borders of magnificent sullen blacks and reds, so that the sun might set it ablaze. He would plant sentinel trees to guard his garden, sentinels such as coppery red crabapple, *Malus* 'Profusion', and the dark-foliaged flowering cherry, *Prunus cerasifera* 'Nigra'. *M.* 'Profusion', with its black-red foliage, would smother itself in season with masses of deep red, slightly fragrant flowers, followed by small fruit the colour of oxblood. *P. c.* 'Nigra' would sport purple-red tonings on its boot-button black leaves, and the Black Knight, who is, on the whole, a tolerant fellow, would turn a blind eye to its single pink blossoms in spring.

A knight so bold would require lashings of drama in his garden; he would therefore plant masses of the ruby-wine cabbage tree, *Cordyline* 'Purple Tower'. Beneath their spiky swords, he would perhaps plant shrubs such as the smoke bush, *Cotinus coggygria* 'Royal Purple' and *Berberis thunbergii* 'Atropurpurea'. Their maroon-black foliage would please him, and he would rejoice in autumn when they burst into flame as though a pyromaniac had set their hearts ablaze. He would not be able to resist a planting nearby of *Geranium psilostemon*; caught in a shaft of sunlight, the flowers' bold black eyes, fringed with magenta-red, glow with an incredible intensity.

Perhaps he would approve of the glowing copper-red of the new foliage on *Photinia* 'Red Robin', and the small shrub *Nandina domestica pygmaea* would please him with wonderful tones of plum, fiery reds and crimson. The compact native *Weinmannia* 'Kiwi Red' could add its glow with garnet and ruby foliage. For further drama, a total change of foliage texture and form could be given by the dwarf *Pittosporum tenuifolium* 'Tom Thumb', with amethyst-black glossy leaves which have the bonus of attractive undulating margins.

There is little doubt that the Black Knight would punctuate his shrubs with generous plantings of his namesake, *Phormium tenax* 'Black Knight', for its dark bronze-black architectural foliage, and to complement it, he would perhaps choose the dwarf. *P. t. rubrum*, which burns with deep coppery red spikes and overtones of rosy russets. Though somewhat moody, the Black Knight has a soft heart, and this gentleness would be revealed in plantings of the delicate maples *Acer palmatum* 'Atropurpureum', and *A. p.* 'Red Pygmy', chosen for their leaves like burgundy lace and dusky palmate fans.

The flowers in this warrior's garden would be strong in form and bold in colour. Great clumps of day lilies, *Hemerocallis* 'Oriental Ruby', 'Alcazar' and 'Riley Baron', would make statements of flame and cinnabar. *H.* 'Ed Murray' would delight him, with near-black ruffled petals rising from its green throat, and he would absolutely not countenance being without *H.* 'Fifth Symphony', which has luminous velvet ruby-red chalices with a blackish cast and a heart of chartreuse.

In autumn, dahlias such as 'Fire Mountain' and 'Bishop of Llandaff hair' would give his autumn garden bronze-black foliage and bold blooms of ruddy red, and for winter no self-respecting Black Knight would be without the camellia 'Night Rider'. This last will warm the colder days with red-black waxen flowers burnished with golden stamens, and new foliage of oriental lacquered coral.

The bold forms and foliage of the iris would be cherished in this garden of strong design. The Black Knight's namesake would again be repeated in plantings of *Iris chrysographes* 'Black Knight'. We might also find this flower emblazoned perhaps upon his personal standard or livery. There would be *Iris mellita* and *I.* 'Chocolate Fish' with burgundy-red flowers, *I.* 'Royal

Trumpeter', velvet maroon with bronze heart, *I*. 'Dutch Chocolate', rich brownish red, and the curious black-hearted *Hermodactylus tuberosus*, the widow or snake's head iris.

The flowers of *Salvia splendens* 'Burning Embers', of unique reddish maroon would be welcome in this garden, as would the old favourite *Lobelia cardinalis* 'Queen Victoria', with beetroot-coloured foliage and red-lead blooms. The Black Knight would use clumps of aromatic rosy purple-leaved sage to enhance their rusty warmth.

Unlike some gardeners, who shall remain nameless, he would be strong enough to conquer chocoholic tendencies, and have scrumptious patches of the bitter-chocolate-coloured and scented *Cosmos atrosanguineus*. Best of all, he could have great flower towers of hollyhocks with single flowers as black as witching hour. At their feet could rest pansies and violas, as many as could be crammed in, with faces of midnight velvet, and a border of the jet-black mondo grass, *Ophiopogon japonicus*.

The Black Knight, as we have discussed, is really quite a softie at his smouldering dark heart. He would give passionate thought to the cultivation of roses with which to woo his lady with chivalry and in the best romantic tradition. He would gather great armfuls of the sumptuous black-red 'Étoile de Hollande' and hurl its petals of velvet at her feet as he galloped past on his charger, or of the beautifully formed deep claret blooms of 'Souvenir du Dr Jamain'. Perhaps for very special occasions he would bring her just one perfect long stem of maroon-red 'Guinée', perfect in bud, flower and scent. If he were a present-day knight he would most certainly woo her with madly extravagant bouquets of David Austin's 'Dark Lady', of deepest, darkest red, gorgeous with the fully open peony blooms which are scattered across wallpapers and fabrics of yesteryear, and possessed of all their old fragrance.

If I were the Black Knight's lady, I should ask for the roses in my lord's garden to be underplanted with oceans of blood-red wallflowers, such as 'Red King' and 'Bloody Warrior', so that their dark velvet petals would lull the bees on summer's breath, and fill the air with piercing sweetness after showers of rain. The raindrops would lie on their petals of ruby velvet like a web of trembling diamonds.

If our sombre crusader could find a little time apart from his flowers, his jousting and various wars, he might indulge his appreciation of fine wines by producing some from his own estate. He could enclose his fiery garden with a backdrop of the stunning purple-leaved grape *Vitis vinifera* 'Atropurpurea'. His serfs would harvest them, treading the fruit in great wooden vats until their dark blood flowed with sweet intoxicating fragrance.

Our Black Knight would perhaps instruct the serfs in the cultivation of a small *jardin potager* (cook's garden) where he could potter, admiring his plump red tomatoes, sweet red peppers and crimson capsicums, fiery chillies, plum-black aubergines, rosy radishes and rows of the frilly auburn heads of lettuce 'Lollo Rossa Foxy'.

But all this talk of flowers and fruit must cease, the battle begin. The scene is set. The board shall be the white section of a garden, Elizabethan in design, in Northland. The players are in position. The White Queen lowers her pale head and returns an icy smile to the Black Knight's sullen and smouldering glances. Is my courage equal to his? Can I banish her flowers of pearl and silver, and replace them with his of blackest red, of Stygian darkness, of opulent fiery warmth and dark magnificence?

CHAPTER TWENTY-FIVE

A SPRING
TOUR

Spring is the season which has moved writers, poets, gardeners and artists down the centuries to ecstatic prose, poetry, planting and works of art. It is the time when, no matter how old we are, we are filled with the sense of wonder at the miracle of regeneration, which remains undiminished, no matter how many times we have seen the process before.

Spring brings a sense of excitement, a hush in the garden, a breathless momentous pause before the rising life will suddenly overflow and make an end to winter. We rush outside, longing to be part of the new life burgeoning all around us. Although the practical everyday chores must still be done, it is amazing how quickly one can get through them when spring is in the air.

Today, as I did my animal rounds, my intoxication with the perfect September morning communicated itself to the cattle, and they shifted paddocks at breakneck speed, kicking up their heels in a most unmatronly fashion, happy to indulge in a spot of spring fever with me. The round complete, I raced back to the house for breakfast, and became queen of the 'jiffy housewives' in my haste to get out into the garden – I might miss something. I am mindful of the very definite rules for making 'The Grand Tour' as commanded by Beverley Nichols, writing in his book *Down the Garden Path* in 1932:

> *The chief rule is that you must never take anything out of its order. You may be longing to see if a crocus has come out in the orchard, but it is strictly forbidden to look before you have inspected all the beds, bushes and trees that lead up to the orchard. You must not look at the bed ahead before you have finished with the bed immediately in front of you. You may see, out of the corner of your eye, a gleam of strange and unexpected scarlet in the next bed but one, but you must steel yourself against rushing at this exciting blaze, and you must stare with cool eyes at the earth in front, which is apparently black, until you have made certain that it is not hiding anything. Otherwise you will find that you rush wildly round the garden, discover one or two sensational events, and decide that nothing else has happened. Which means that you miss all the thrill of tiny shoots, the first lifting of the lids of the wallflowers, the first precious gold of the witch-hazel, or the early spear of the snowdrop . . .*

I found it quite easy to linger for a thorough inspection of the early roses which are already in bloom in our subtropical (well, usually) Northland climate. 'Souvenir de Madame Léonie Viennot' is already smothered with coppery pink blooms, which are embroidered through with an amethyst haze of pendulous wisteria. They are the most perfect of companions, and are the haunt of bees and garden visitors with cameras. The dainty rose 'Frühlingsmorgen' fulfils her name 'Spring Morning', already proclaiming the season begun with golden yellow flowers above ferny foliage. *Rosa* 'Canary Bird' is opening lemon-yellow single flowers too, which smell of honey, and 'Old Blush', not to be outdone as another harbinger of spring, cascades soft pink blooms from the top of a rose pole.

One of my favourite sights at this time of year is the new foliage on the rosebushes – all ruby reds, burgundies and clarets

— so new, so glossy, so healthy, so perfect. I always long to freeze such foliage in a moment of time. All the bushes are massed with tightly furled buds in promise of glory to come, but I think it might be pleasant to have half the bushes in flower, and the other half still sporting this intoxicating alcoholic haze of foliage colour.

Another early rose in bloom is the Rugosa 'Blanc Double de Coubert', which has exquisite virginal blooms of purest white, with an intensely fragrant perfume. This rose has semi-double petals which are so fine and translucent it used to be called the 'Muslin Rose'. In parts of Europe it is much used in bridal bouquets and head-dresses.

Moving slowly and carefully as bidden by Mr Nichols, I visit the tree lawn next, to indulge in a great orgy of 'sniffing', gathering bouquets of fragrant 'paper white' narcissi to scent the house, and inhaling again and again the rich scent of the white goblets of the Yulan magnolia. They have burst out of their furry sepals, which now cup them from below like rabbits' ears. The arms of the other trees are wearing sleeves of green lace as a mist of tiny new leaves unfold to the spring sunshine.

From the tree lawn, I can see that the ponga around the water gardens are unfurling lacey new fronds of soft yellow-gold, their tribute to the new season. Near the pond also is a sight which I look forward to each year, for this is the time when the native *Clematis paniculata* festoons an old tree with starry white blossoms which are mirror-imaged on the face of the water. The Maori call this flower 'Puawhananga' – 'the sacred flower' – and when we see it in the bush we know that spring is well and truly here.

The rules allow me to wander onwards, to stand beneath the old kahikatea tree near the *Acer* garden. It is hung in clouds and clouds of other varieties of cascading clematis stars, the whole sky seems full of flowers. I become quite giddy with star-gazing and decide I'd better finish the 'Grand Tour' and do some work.

One of the most immutable of gardening laws is that for every flower, there are twenty weeds greeting the new season with their own form of exuberance and generosity.

It is difficult to write about spring without using all the old clichés – the season of hope and faith; the time of gapey-mouthed insistent fledglings, downy golden ducklings; of prancing lambs and late calves struggling to rise on long unsteady legs; of massed bulbs, daffodils and narcissi, beneath the trees in the orchard – but all *are* the very fabric of this most joyous of the seasons.

On a more prosaic level, it is said that the first sign of spring is the whirr of the lawnmower, and already I can hear my neighbour using his. I begin my weeding with a light heart, luxuriating in the warmth of the new sun on my back, thinking how good it is to have the whole new garden season ahead; to be able to look forward to welcoming, like old friends, the well-loved plants which will bloom each to their month.

On this early spring morning the first flowers I find blooming in the beds are the smaller ones – violets, whole sheets of merry little 'Johnny-jump-up' violas, jewelled polyanthus, *Primula malacoides* blooming tiny flowers in tiers like miniature candelabras, snowdrops, dainty *Linaria* 'Fairy Bouquet', *Ipheion* with star-shaped flowers a pale watercolour wash of blue.

The bolder, deeper blue of the flowers showing on the clumps of *Iris unguicularis* is delightful, and always surprises me. This Algerian iris seems so exotic a flower against its unprepossessing dwarf leaf spikes when it bursts into bloom, often as early as mid-winter. In the Northland warmth the *Antirrhinum* 'Madame Butterfly' is already unfolding frilly wings, and self-sown *Cineraria* flowers blaze from odd corners in singing pinks and purples. They are considered a little vulgar by some, but coming on the heels of so many grey days, such vibrant colour is welcome.

The veranda is drenched with the perfume of the pink and white stars of *Jasminum polyanthum*. Her companion, the old rose 'Mme Alfred Carrière' is thrusting blush-tipped buds through the jasmine's glossy dissected foliage, soon to delight with white-pink blooms. It is as though the smaller flowers come first, to quicken our anticipation for the floral carnival of riotous bloom, colour and scent which the coming of spring will explode upon our senses.

The finale of my Grand Tour takes me to the orchard, but it is more the symphony of birdsong than flowers which draws me here, though I pause to see how the *Prunus* and fruit trees tease with fat clusters of blossoms, each with the merest whisper of colour at their tips. Thrushes and blackbirds flute loving ballads of piercing sweetness to their mates, and some are already rushing to and fro, collecting small twigs, feathers and other nesting materials. The chaffinch's song soars to a pinnacle, then rushes in silvery scales headlong down again, contrasting with the tui's echoing cadences of mimicry. We have one with pretensions of becoming an opera singer – he or she sings only 'Figaro, Figaro, Figaro!'

The canaries in the aviary are almost bursting their throats in an ecstasy of trilling, whistling song of such volume I can hear it from the orchard. I think that, like me, they are feeling how good, how very good it is to be alive, to have the good fortune to be standing in the heart of a garden on a perfect spring morning. They sing, perhaps as Rilke sang, 'Spring has returned and the earth is like a child that knows poems.'

CHAPTER TWENTY-SIX

ALL ON
A SUMMER'S EVE

Since no one has invented a motormower with headlamps on, I have had (reluctantly) to leave the fragrance of the newly mown grass in the summer twilight and come indoors where the great heat of the day still lingers.

It was beautiful in the garden this evening as the light faded. The most wonderful of sights was nine of my white fantail pigeons on the brilliant flaming-red flower bracts of *Bougainvillea* 'Scarlet O'Hara', their snowy feathers making a vivid contrast against the scarlet bracts with the tiny white eyes.

The magic of the midsummer evening was down at the pond too. Labradors Missy and Amber had been swimming. They had shaken large droplets of water onto the huge silvery plates of the lotus leaves, and January's New Year moon was just touching both them and the great creamy flowerheads with her light. Seven tiny fantails were darting around the fronds of the branches trailing in the pool, cheeping in delight as they swooped and took their fill of the insects imprudent enough to be staying out so late at night. I stood very still for a while, not wanting human movement to disturb this private magic of bird flight and just-born moonlight.

Beneath the trailing branches at the rear of the great willow is my retreat. I have cut them back to head height and put inside this cool and green, gloomy cavern two old chairs which make my secret hideout for when the phone rings too much, or I am visitor weary. Batteries are recharged in ten minutes as I lift my eyes to the bush-clad mountain shimmering in the summer heat from my possie of delicious cool.

In the tangled brown hair of a young matai tree in a large dragon pot, a thrush has nested, housing her babies in a superb waterside apartment. I part the branches gently as I pass (knowing Mum is away poaching the evening snails) to check they are not in danger of falling into the pond, and resolve to place a safety-belt of chicken wire around their deluxe apartment next morning.

I cannot leave the pond without pausing to admire a favourite corner fast disappearing into the twilight. I planted here powder-blue lacecap hydrangeas, silvery hostas and tall white iris, to reflect into the water. I disturb the bullfrogs meditating on the lotus leaves and they leap angrily into the water, shattering the flower images into a mosaic of blue and white.

As I come back up into the Elizabethan garden the air is drowsy with the scent of the old roses, and I think of Empress Josephine walking in her rose gardens at Malmaison so long ago, on such an evening, before she returned to the pomp and ceremony of court and, of course, to her Napoleon. I think, too, of poor condemned Anne Boleyn in her cell above the Tower gardens. Did the scent of the first roses of spring ease her despair perhaps a little, and distract her sad thoughts?

I make my way reluctantly to the vege garden to pull a crinkly-coated lettuce for my supper. Here, a great fat rabbit is tasting one in advance for me, but so lovely is the evening, I forgive him. My doves swoop down from the peach and nectarine trees in the orchard, taking advantage of my lingering footsteps in the gardens to scrounge a last handful of grain for their supper. I have one particularly loving one who snuggles into the side of my neck and oversees my gardening activities until she tires of her wobbly perch, which just does not have time enough to stand still for her.

This year's calves — my hand-reared babies such a short time ago — chunky little beasts now, race around the paddock doing their mad-calf act as a final salute to the day. They thunder to the orchard fence to see if I will throw them over a last barrowload of weeds as relief from the drought-stricken paddocks. I tell them 'No such luck' and bid them goodnight.

Back at the house I see that the labradors, wreckers of waterlilies, are stretched full length on the verandas, cooling off after another hard day supervising the inexplicable activities of the humans and life on the farm.

Yesterday I found two tiny turkey babies who had been left behind by their careless mother as she went up to the top paddocks. They were too weak to follow her, so I am having to hand-rear them. Not an easy job, as they will starve themselves to death rather than eat. I have to force-feed them a ground-up mixture of tiny seeds, dog meat and grain. They shake their beaks vigorously after every beakful, to try to get rid of the filthy food — boy, what a mess! The anorexic ones are now cuddled up in an old woolly bobble hat in the airing cupboard, whispering to each other in their pretty little voices about the iniquity of humans who force-feed one.

Indulging in a last glance through the windows at the now almost invisible gardens, I lament the passing of the pansies, and the daisy bushes I so cruelly cut back today, but rejoice at the large lemon chalices of the evening primrose flowers still visible and luminous in the last light of day. To bath, to wash away the heat and labours of the day with the delicious fragrance of the wild-rose soap, bath oil and talc the husband and daughter gave me for Christmas, and to plan the next day's toil in the gardens and on the farm . . .

*It would indeed be very wise to leave many parts of the grass
unmown for the sake of growing many beautiful plants. . . .
we want carpets of grass here and there, but what a nuisance
it is to shave it as often as foolish men shave their faces! . . .
Who would not rather see the waving grass with countless
flowers than a close surface without a blossom. . .*

William Robinson,
The Wild Garden

CHAPTER TWENTY-SEVEN

THE PERFECT
GARDENER

Collapsing in a hot and dishevelled heap this sweltering mid-January afternoon, beneath the shade of a peach tree, I ask myself just why I have been crawling around wrenching unyielding weeds from beds and borders of concrete clay. Leaning my aching back against the cool trunk of the tree, and wiping away the beads of perspiration trickling into my eyes, the answer to the question comes with stern self-reprimand. If my garden labour programme were properly organised, I should not now be a sodden, exhausted heap, but working quietly and efficiently away at some non-strenuous chore like dead-heading the roses in a cool, shaded area of the garden. Furthermore, the whopping weeds wouldn't have been there in the first place had a timely labour schedule eliminated them *before* they broke out into luxurious seedheads and self-sowed with such generosity all over the garden.

One of the labradors, panting, fugitive also from the torpid afternoon, joins me in the green shades of my retreat, laying her head across my lap. Settling more comfortably against the tree trunk, my thoughts wander away in a contemplation of the Perfect Garden. It is an agreeable dream.

The first requirement, of course, would be a Perfect

Gardener. This garden person would never have a sunburned, peeling nose, calloused, soil-ingrained hands with no fingernails, because he or she would absolutely not be seen dead on a broiling afternoon without sunblock, wide-brimmed hat and cool cotton work gloves. They would never have allowed themselves to be in the position of having to weed in a temperature soaring into the thirties because they would have annihilated undesirables as soon as they dared raise their heads above ground. Should a few have escaped their eagle eyes, these admirable persons would have pulled them smartly and with ease after a shower of rain, or when the sprinkler had moistened the area nicely. How absurd, they would titter, at the very notion of *any* gardener found trying to hoe concrete clay in February.

It is unthinkable that the Perfect Garden Person would ever be heard muttering barrack-room oaths and playing demented, time-wasting games of 'hunt the trowel or secateurs'. They would never have mislaid them, thrown them away in a barrowload of plant refuse or planted them in the compost bins. They would not do this because their tools would be tucked snugly into one of those sensible kangaroo pouches upon their persons. In the unlikely event that they should mislay these tools (purely momentarily, of course), they would have a second one of each to hand, to put into instant action until the first set turned up, thereby saving time and eliminating the risk of high blood pressure.

I examine these expensive pouches in garden centres – until I am seduced by a bigger, better, brighter or more repeat-blooming plant, which I know would look simply stunning in *my* garden. Which leads me further up the path of failed intentions – *where* in my garden? The Perfect Garden Person would never succumb to the impulse buying of a plant which would cause them to wander around with it in their hands for a week, wondering where on earth to put it. They would adhere with admirable self-restraint to the golden rule of buying 'a plant for a place', so that they would not waste ages trying to find 'a place for a plant'. They would have it popped in, all blooming beautiful in minutes. They would absolutely never, ever have to dig out another plant, or give one a 'long ride in the wheelbarrow' to make room for the impulse buy.

It is logical also to suppose that the Perfect Gardener, before planting anything, would measure out on the earth the plant's exact full-grown dimensions, and simply never dream of planting anything in all that lovely (temporary) bare space. They would laugh uproariously at the idea of planting too much too close in the first place. They would not end up in a couple of years with an impenetrable shrubbery in which the army could hold jungle warfare manoeuvres and which requires hours of exhausting hacking with a machete, and brutal pruning to stay its advance on the perennial borders.

He or she would make careful study of the soil and aspect of their garden before planting anything. They would then plant (having prepared and enriched the soil first with compost from a discreet, well-rotted heap behind the garden shed) only those plants which would adore it there and thrive with rude health. The Perfect Gardener would not for one moment entertain the idea of wasting money, time and energy trying to coax fragile, fascinating beauties like the blue Himalayan poppy to grow in crude clay which is a quagmire in winter and a pickaxe job in summer. He or she would blush with shame if they saw a *Plants I Have Murdered* list like mine.

In this Perfect Garden all the perennials and especially the old roses with obscure and tongue-twisting names would be clearly labelled so that its owner would never suffer embarrassing bouts of *Hortus botanicus amnesia* when asked for them by visitors. It goes without saying that he or she would also be so organised that all the garden chores would be complete before guests arrived, leaving time to clean up, change and sally forth in immaculate, trendy denim garden gear. They would positively sneer at the thought of lobbing barrows and tools in the general direction of the shed and sprinting, filthy and dishevelled, for the bathroom as visitors' cars come up the drive.

This admirable person would have a meticulous plan for successive plantings for continuous year-round colour and interest. They would not, like me, be staring moodily from my place of refuge from the sun's zenith at large, bare spaces in the borders where annuals have gasped, keeled over and expired. These would be generously underplanted with perennials and bulbs, lined up and just waiting to spring forth into dazzling glory. The Perfect Gardener would choose not to believe that there are actually those among us who will rush out and embezzle the housekeeping on plants 'for instant colour'.

It needs little imagination to guess that the flowerbeds and borders in this garden would have beautifully worked out colour schemes in three or four harmonising tones. The owner would suffer no hesitation whatsoever in ripping out some gay but incorrectly coloured plant which has had the effrontery to self-sow. He or she would not be weak enough to let such plants win and turn the white and silver, or the lavender, pink and blue beds into a multi-coloured brocade. Vulgar dahlias of hot orange, acid-yellow marigolds, bedding plants of vile bonfire reds and screaming pinks would not be entertained, and all plantings would be in refined, genteel hues.

The Perfect Garden would never invite in screaming winds and shattering rain to devastate its perfection, it would never smother itself in mud and become a wild, tangled monster. It would invite in only gentle amounts of steady rain, which would fall mostly at night. Only gentle breezes to cool the heat of day would be admitted, and all, just all, the taller perennials and roses would have been firmly staked against the weather, so that they would not be keeling over like ninepins and lying face down in the mud.

Kamikaze bugs, slugs, pests, all varieties of fungus and mildew which might just manage to creep in, these would keep a very low profile and be desperately well behaved. They would soon flip over and wave their legs in the air because they would succumb to the Perfect Gardener's highly efficient and deadly pest-control programme. He or she would have listened carefully to the weather forecast before spraying, of course; this way, they would never be heard cursing because a downpour had washed off all that expensive spray ten minutes after it has been applied.

The daydream is suddenly less agreeable. Contemplation of life in the Perfect Garden is becoming more exhausting than the brassy heat of the Northland afternoon. Sheer defiance in the face of the paragon of the person who is its gardener inclines me to idle longer. I am a willing captive to the sleeping dog's head in my lap, and to the heat-drenched scent of the roses near my shaded green bower.

Because I am very much less than a Perfect Gardener I can lie and watch the bees, legs dusted with gold pollen, bumbling in and out of the blue and pink-washed *Echium* flowers. I can smile at the jewelled flashes of brilliance which are the Rosella parakeets flashing into the tree above my head to feast on its fruit. I can share it with them; simply by reaching up my hand I can enjoy the sensuous pleasure of picking and eating a golden sun-warmed peach.

I can lean back, close my eyes and listen to the liquid cadences and arpeggios of the tuis as they practise their scales. I can make an in-depth study of the stunning beauty of a vermilion-pink peony bloom of the Rugosa rose, 'Roseraie de l'Hay'. I can marvel at the thick boss of golden stamens at its heart, and at the delicate transparency of tissue-paper petals above deeply veined hardy foliage of darkest moss-green. I can breathe my fill of the rose's essential oils which, released by the sun, make its exquisite old-world fragrance.

Because I am less than a perfect gardener, weeds have seeded, the lawns have not been mown before they need mowing, the hedges have not been clipped before they need clipping, so there will be endless barrowloads of both to spread and compost. I am still grubby and sunburned, dressed like a refugee from a charity shop, sticky with peach juice and labour, but I am untroubled. I am tranquil, because into my daydreams creeps a certain suspicion – could it be, could it be that both the Perfect Gardener and his or her garden might not just be desperately, desperately boring?

> *I wouldn't want to make it look like a gardener's garden, all clipped an' spick an' span, would you?' said Dickon. 'It's nicer like this with things runnin' wild, an' swingin' an' catchin' hold of each other.*

Frances Hodgson Burnett,
The Secret Garden

CHAPTER TWENTY-EIGHT

LADIES
OF THE NIGHT

A scene from a steamy movie – a racy novel – of harem beauties floating by in wisps of chiffon? Afraid not; this tale is of ladies of another species, who play hermit to the sun, of a journey into darkness, and nocturnal adventure.

Last night I could not sleep and, tired of tossing and turning in our humid Northland night, I took a drink out into the delicious dark cool on the veranda. I sat for only a short while before I was drawn into the garden which lay secret and silent in summer moonlight.

The thought came of how well we all know our gardens of sunlight, but how little we know of their magic and mystery at night. Dusk brings to each of us a second garden, cloaking the bright colours of the day with shadow harmonies of peaceful dove-greys, silver, lemons, pearly whites, and velvet-blacks of ebony and jet.

As I watched, the stars seemed to burst and bubble, to keep quiet vigil with the night-blooming flowers. Flat white and pastel-pale by day, they undergo a moonlight metamorphosis, reborn as 'ladies of the night', wearing an iridescent pearly sheen and wafting wanton perfumed breath upon the cool night air.

These ladies are described as 'vespertine' – of evening – or 'crepuscular' – coming with twilight. They court lovers among the ghostly, ethereal moths and insects that unfurl wings of silver gauze only after the sun has gone down. They are the night pollinators, the ladies' nocturnal courtiers, with whom they hold moonlit trysts. I watched these insects flitting silently among the green-white opalescent bells of night-scented *Nicotiana langsdorfii* and *N. affinis*. Nature has her night world filled with insects and animals which have slept away the hours of sunlight.

As my feet made shadowed imprints in the soft wet grass, I experienced, in my romantic moonlit interlude, the dubious pleasure of treading barefoot on fat, slimy slugs. I hoped the hedgehog I had seen earlier, bumbling and snuffling its way around, would follow my footsteps and dine royally on the slugs and snails silvering the grass with crystalline trails.

Enchanted by the shining waterfall foliage of the weeping silver pear, *Pyrus salicifolia*, I sat for a while and listened to the sounds of the night. In nature, there is rarely utter silence; in the heart of the garden in the depths of the country, the short intervals of silence seemed profound but were soon broken by the morepork's haunting requiem or by the breeze, swishing through the treetops. It stirred a patch of flat seedpods, ghosts of long-gone honesty flowers, into dry, rasping whispers. Each pod looked like a miniature moon in the half light. Beyond the sigh of the wind, there was the slow, companionable breathing of the cattle on the other side of the fence.

From the pond area, the 'froggies who would a-wooing go' croaked solemnly and fell with hollow plops into the pool. The quiet face of the moon rested in calm water, among the creamy lotuses' and water lilies' waxen petals. We have all sheltered gratefully beneath the cool green canopies of ponga umbrellas in the heat of the day, but how different is their form at night. The great fronds of the tree ferns surrounding the pool made filigree patterns like Victorian lace, sweeping across the surface of the silvered water, a sight of great beauty.

Leaving the pool, I was drawn towards the vege garden by the magnificent spiked foliage of the globe artichoke, *Cynara scolymus*, tower blocks of ghostly felted silver in the moonlight. Nearby, in the flower garden, equally dramatic, were the huge heads of the tall architectural *Nicotiana sylvestris*, which seemed to explode in the darkness in a catherine wheel of ivory exclamation marks, hurling perfume of spiced honey to drench the night air. In the Elizabethan Garden, the tiny white flowers of *Gypsophila* and *Coriander* had become patches of milky froth, making the sundial they surrounded look as though it were floating as it counted the moon's hours.

The ivory towers made by my white foxgloves reminded me of how, when I was a child, I was told by my grandfather that they were the fairies' flowers. I remember how many of their bell heads I picked, peering intently into each freckled cup, searching for the elusive creatures. Velvet moths are their secret occupants now, and I, much older and perhaps wiser, am in possession of the more certain knowledge that the magic is in the flowers themselves.

This magic shone from the flowers of a patch of delicate Japanese anemones, 'windflowers' gleaming with pale ethereal purity, as the moonlight rippled from behind a banner of cloud. But the stars of my night garden had to be the simple white shasta and marguerite daisies. In full moonlight they became luminous tracts of stars gleaming in galaxies of ivory and gold. Towering above them, the tall evening primrose, *Oenothera lamarckiana*, whose blooms are tightly furled whispers of faded satin beneath the sun, had opened pale lemon chalices which seemed to have captured the last light of day, to be reflected joyfully into the dusky air. Their scent was elusive and sweet, unlike that of the night-scented stock, *Matthiola bicornis*, which drenched the air with intense perfume nearby. In the warmth of the day, its pale lilac flowers droop unhappily, but when the sun sets, it revives to become a leading lady of the night. So, too, does the old-fashioned *Mignonette odorata*, whose reseda-coloured bristle flowers are insignificant by day but powerfully fragrant at night.

Sunshine and daylight had combined to release the powerful aromatic oils of many of the culinary plants in the herb garden, and their piquant perfumes distilled into the warm night air teased the nostrils. The old English herb, 'sweet rocket', *Hesperis matrionalis* – 'mother of the night' – threw up luxuriant spires of massed small lilac flowers. She was the *femme fatale* of the herb garden, with a fragrance so intensely sweet she was besieged by winged suitors. The most pungent of aromas, evoking memories of heat-filled Mediterranean nights (or pizza parlours nearer home) wafted from the fleshy oregano-scented leaves of 'allherb' or 'five flavours herb', *Coleus amboinicus*.

Soon my journey around the moonlit garden was almost over, and, leaving the spicy fragrance of the herbs, a last delight was to linger beneath the trellis to look at the pearled loveliness of the old roses in the half-light. The perfume of the yellow pink-flushed flowers of the honeysuckle, *Lonicera periclymenum*, tumbled among them caused me to linger, and the statuette of a mother and child who live in this lovely bower welcomed me with gentle alabaster smiles.

It seemed that the scents of the night were more exotic than those of the sun-drenched day. They reminded me of the incomparable perfume of the prima donna of all the night flowers, the moon cactus, *Hylocereus undatus*. I grew this plant in pots during my 'thwarted gardener' days, in a tiny balcony-garden in a high-rise tower block in Hong Kong. It was a drab, unattractive plant for most of the year, until it suddenly produced great elongated oyster-coloured buds. My family and I would sit entranced, watching them slowly unfurl about midnight, like time-lapse photography, into huge exotic white blooms with golden stamens at their hearts. The powerful tropical perfume of just one flower was enough to drench the night air, the balcony and our tiny flat. We were reluctant to cease our moonflower gazing and go to bed, knowing that by morning the exquisite ephemeral flowers would be folded parasols of crushed silk.

With this memory, my nocturnal garden tour was complete, and I returned to bed tranquil, grateful for the beauty and scent of the night-blooming flowers. Drifting to sleep, I made a mental list of the ladies of the night I would plant around the barbecue, veranda and entertaining areas of the garden.

I dreamed of sipping a glass of chilled wine with friends on moonlit summer evenings while we contemplated the languorous, moon-glided ladies with their sensuous perfume and ghostly radiance. I cannot remember who said the purpose of the garden is for rejoicing the eye and refreshing the spirit – but I know now that its ethereal beauty by moonlight is guaranteed to turn even the most log-like of sleepers into moon-gazing insomniacs. Try it and see.

> *. . . No evening scents, I think, have the fascination of the evening primrose, especially that of the commonest variety. Those pale moons irradiate the twilight with their sweet elusive perfumes.*
>
> Eleanour Sinclair-Rhode,
> *The Scented Garden*

CHAPTER TWENTY-NINE

AUTUMN AND THE COMING OF THE RAINS

If a gardener were playing a word-association game, it is certain that after the word 'autumn' he or she would reply 'colour'. For autumn is a soft and silky creature, gentle and restful after the hard brilliance of summer. She comes brown-skinned, bounteous with harvest gifts, dressed in crimson-reds, molten golds and beaten copper, but the foliage of her garments is tattered and ragged.

She brings mellow days of Indian summer, and mysterious mornings shrouded in mist. They are made luminous by a spectral sun seeping in from behind, so that the gloom has brilliance of its own. A mist shrouded the garden this morning so thick that the cobwebs drooped heavy and hoar as though they had been knitted with wool. Summer passes and before we have consciously relinquished it, suddenly it is autumn. There is a chill in the air, the world turns crimson and gold, the sun follows a shorter arc, nights grow cold, the air grows clearer and the enervating humidity of summer is lost.

For many of us, the greatest gift autumn brings is the end of the parched months of summer drought. Today, the first real rains of the season came in a dramatic thunderstorm, all tumbled through with rainbows. The storm began with pelting rain, tip-tapping a thousand fingertips across the iron roof, then it came sheeting down in great fat drops, causing gutterings and spouts to overflow, and the small creeks which have been silent all summer to gurgle and murmur again.

Thunder rumbled and boomed as the storm unrolled, the wind crashed through the treetops, and it sounded as though everything up above had fallen on the floor of the sky. The dogs, trembling, sought refuge against my legs, seeking reassurance in the face of this almost-forgotten phenomenon.

Strings of rain hissed on the drive, and the doves and pigeons indulged in an orgy of ablutions, lifting first one wing and then the other, exposing armpits to the cool, cleansing streams, as it washed away the dust and heat of summer. They ruffled their feathers, embracing the silver kisses of the rain.

The veil of flying water washes all, and it is as though the weary soil, grass and gardener breathe again. The garden shines with silver vapour, and the birds shout loud messages of delight and excitement from the trees' sheltering arms. The rain eases to soft silent threads, no longer a deluging torrent but quiet showers. The clouds part, the sun slants across the threads severing them, and everything shines cool and crystal clean.

The dogs and I are happy that the storm has lost its fury and are delighted with the rain. We walk through the wet Elizabethan Garden, the wet rose gardens, the wet vege gardens, the wet Birds Garden, and through the wet, wet water gardens. We are prepared to be shocked by whatever devastation the storm has wreaked, but apart from the heads of the tall chrysanthemums which hang earthwards, heavy with raindrops, all is well, and the earth smells deliciously moist and fragrant.

Perhaps autumn appeals more to our senses of taste and smell than the other seasons. The dogs and I took refuge in the kitchen during the deluge, and there it smelled as though a caravaner's spice wagon had passed this way in the night. The scents of cinnamon, ginger, pepper, garlic, allspice, nutmegs and cloves tingle in the nostrils, and flavour the contents of the jars stacked so satisfyingly on the cupboard shelves, against winter malnourishment.

With autumn's munificent harvest of ripened fruit I have been making chutneys and jams, and the air is sweet and sour! Onions are being pickled (mostly in my tears), tomatoes relished, and fruit boiled in the big preserving pan on the stove for jams and jellies of luscious reds and purples.

I think autumn is the best season for wholesome smells. The rich, cloying flower scents of summer's cavalcade have gone, and in their place are tangy, mellow smells – fruit smells, apples, pears and persimmons; chrysanthemums, mouldering leaves and vegetation, damp-earth smells, garden refuse smouldering in bonfires, and the comforting smell of logs burning in pot-bellied stoves. There are fresh sawdust smells from pruned tree limbs, and rich decaying odours from the manure spread to prepare the earth for spring. There is no other smell quite like that of an earth-damp mushroom, nor like the feel of the cool freshness of its pearly stem and cap in the fingers.

Autumn has its own sounds, too. The air no longer hums with the voice of lawnmowers, but with that of chainsaws cutting logs for winter fires. There is the sudden whirr of pheasants' wings, the frantic cries of ducks as they flee the hunter's gun and the excited chatters of a thousand birds in the trees, and on the telegraph wires, as they anticipate the moment of beginning their vast migratory journeys. There is the sound of fruit falling in the orchard with hollow plops, and of the blackbirds and thrushes crashing about, plundering whatever is still left on the trees.

As I walked in the warm, wet garden, I hoped the chrysanthemums of rich autumnal colours of bronze, copper, gold and dusky reds would dry soon. They take over admirably from the fading dahlias in the floral parade, and their earthy, spicy fragrance seems to embody the very essence of the season. A kind garden visitor gave me some cuttings of a dwarf chrysanthemum of unknown name (which I am still researching) and it has given me much joy. Its flowers have hearts of the warmest gold, surrounded by petals of a deep velvet claret-red. The blooms mass themselves so thoroughly that the foliage is lost – they are my jewels of autumn. At the back of the beds, asters flaunt impudent fringes of mauvy pinks and purples, and the early-blooming sasanqua camellias are already unfolding rosy blossoms to the balmy air.

Autumn is not only John Keats's 'season of mists and mellow fruitfulness'; it is also the time when many plants proffer the gift of a second blooming. Many of the roses flowering now are more beautiful because their petals are not bleached or scorched by the harsh summer sun, and their colours are more intense in the soft autumn light. The hips on the Rugosa roses are magnificent; some are elongated ovals of deepest shiny crimson, and others are fat red globes with whiskered sepals.

The work we put into the autumn garden seems to have something of an act of faith about it – the plantings of shrubs, trees and hardy seeds. No matter how many times I sow my rows of broad beans, I can scarcely believe that the seeds will germinate in the heavy wet soil. We cover tender plants with frost cloth and commit bulbs to the earth, all acts of faith, because we know that, though their life is dormant now, it must be protected in order that it might live yet more abundantly in the future.

Even the endless clearing-up work – the cutting back, the pruning, the pulling of weeds easily from the soft, damp soil – is not so much a farewell to summer as a preparation for spring. I admit to feeling a considerable sense of relief each autumn that summer's rampant, engulfing growth is at an end, and that some degree of control may be inflicted upon the garden by the gardener.

Some gardeners find autumn a sad time, but in many ways it is the cradle of spring. It is the time of secret underground growth and germination, and of swelling buds which will all mature through winter days. It is the time when those wicked glossy bulb catalogues arrive in the mail, and when one is drawn towards the shelves in garden centres, unable to resist such sales psychology as invitations to 'fill a bag for only ten dollars'. For me the bulb, like a seed, is nothing short of a miracle. Inside that wrinkled, dry or shiny onion skin is carried all the panoply of green foliage and brilliant flower. I need at least two bags full . . .

Autumn seems to come suddenly, as if a universal drum has been beaten, a silent summons heard. Greens fade rapidly to mellow tones, and the shadows lengthen across the garden. In the mornings the dew is heavy, and when I go out to shift the cattle, it is difficult to tell whether it is dew or frost filming the grass. At noon, it still glistens where the shadows lie and makes a crystal overlay on glistening foliage. Hourly, the deciduous trees seem to change colour more clearly, letting their stippled leaves drift away with reluctance. The foliage of the wisterias and the ginkgo tree becomes rich yellow. Shafts of sunlight, spearing the mist, illuminate the smouldering colour of the liquidambar and pin oak. Their foliage looks stunning against the dark velvet totaras, which are all trussed in cobwebs.

We do not have sufficiently cold temperatures in Northland to make the deciduous trees riot with colour, like those of our neighbours in the South Island, so those that do colour bring great pleasure. The leaves on the persimmon tree in the orchard have changed to delicious burnt-orange, and great conflagrations of flame are leaping from the hearts of the shrubs *Berberis thunbergii* 'Atropurpurea' and *Cotinus coggygria,* the smoke bush.

The foliage of the American dogwoods, especially *Cornus florida* 'Rainbow', also puts on a show of brightest primary colours, come sun or snow. The poplar species we have planted around the farm for land stabilisation and shelter-belt purposes rain down great golden medallions on the backs of the cattle in the paddocks. They raise their heads as if scenting the advance of autumn in the wind.

The loveliness of autumn is ephemeral; its brilliance is one with its fading; its very essence is in its passing. The days shorten, and each one is shorter than its yesterday; the sun weakens and no longer has the strength to climb high and jubilant in the sky; the light becomes soft, suffused with liquid amber.

Autumn should not bring sadness, it is a time of completeness, of the gardening year fulfilled. We know its beauty passes swiftly, but this knowledge gives it the longest life. Because such beauty can endure only in memory, we give it immortality there and keep it forever.

CHAPTER THIRTY

MAY MORNING

Garden visitors came this gentle late May morning. 'Oh,' they said, 'how brave you are to let us come at this time when everything in the garden is so dull, bare and messy.'

Looking, I saw the gaiety of the camellias, the purity of the snowdrops, the bravery of late-blooming roses, early daffodils, drifts of chrysanthemums in their autumnal tints making an early winter brocade. Did the deciduous trees reluctantly drifting down last leaves of gold and crimson with a whisper, and the delicate tracery against the sky of the bare branches and twigs of the silver birches, beneath which I welcomed these visitors, escape their notice? Is the soft gold carpet of leaves on the lawns the mess of which they speak? Are they looking at, without seeing, the great pendulous lavender flowers of the tree dahlia, which has grown to a height of four metres, also silhouetted against the unblemished blue clarity of that winter sky?

Yesterday, perched precariously atop the rose trellis, I indulged in half a reel of film, trying to capture the ecstasy of the bees, murmuring with bumbling intoxication in the thick nectar in the huge gold flower hearts. I can capture their image within the camera, but not their ecstatic drone, nor the fragrance of the flower. But it was fun trying, and I very much enjoyed a bird's-eye view of the bunches of scarlet hips hung on the briars, if not their thorny embrace.

This morning, before the visitors came, the dogs and I stole time enough to go mushrooming, gathering baskets filled to the brim in a rain as soft as cobwebs. How beautiful are their gills of oyster-pink. The visitors rejoiced in punnets to take home with them.

Visitors gone, back to work, musing on a letter from my sister-in-law, Kay, in England, telling me of her joy in seeing the first daffodil and camellia buds, though there were still traces of snow in the sheltered corners of her garden. I am reminded of Shakespeare's observation of 'daffodils that come before the swallows dare, and take the winds of March with beauty'.

The daffodil and camellia buds are swelling here, too, but they are not as furry fat as the great buds forming now on the magnolia trees. Her words remind me of the exquisite fragility of an English spring. I, too, have made ice and snow gardens in Europe, and known the perfect joy of the sight of fringed gold winter aconites like pools of butter, mint-green and pearled snowdrops, and tiny mauve *Anenome blanda*, joyfully throwing off their overcoat of snow.

As spring comes to Kay in the Northern Hemisphere, so comes our winter, but in our 'Winterless North', I wonder if I shall ever get used to the happy-go-lucky nature of the seasons, which seem to lose the separate distinction of those in Europe and merge, with secrets of their own, one into the other. Our spring here in Northland is so unashamedly flamboyant, so beautifully vulgar, as though, with her riotous jumble of bloom and colour, she is apologising for having been away for even so short a time.

But now it is late autumn, the long months of drought broken by the gift of the first blessed rains of winter. The infinite weed seeds, having lain sunbathing all summer long, have germinated (I can hear them growing . . .), greedily sucking up the raindrops. I deliver them foul murder. Autumn-weary annuals receive a stay of execution as I am distracted by a flash of iridescent green – the rare and lovely native New Zealand pigeon, kereru, swooping into the taraire tree above the vege garden, to gorge on the blue-black berries.

I have plied secateurs without mercy; they are hot, the back is breaking. The meditations of the spirit are replaced by the needs of the flesh for a pint-sized mug of tea, and the need to do something about the large batch of ingredients for spiced-apple muffins I left resting on the kitchen table when the visitors came. I have already relieved the old apple tree of its burden by several baskets, and as I take off my boots, I remember that, having lavished a mega-mushroom-omelette on Brian for his breakfast, I have no eggs left in the house.

I will have to go and see if the ladies in the henhouse have been obliging. While I am over there, I can enjoy the dainty creamy primrose bells of the winter-blooming *Clematis tangutica*. And I could just peep at the reflections of the winter sky, and the yellow stems of the bare branches of the great willow, mirror-imaged in the pond. Where is this dull, bare, and messy winter in the garden of which the visitors spake?

CHAPTER THIRTY-ONE

WELCOME, WINTER

I never know whether I am vastly impressed or horrified with my gardening friends who hurl their tools (and work) into the shed, bolt the door and prepare to hibernate totally at the first chill of winter. I am puzzled because winter is a time of evaluation, of learning, when one looks at what has pleased or displeased during the year, a time for rectifying mistakes, for planning and making changes, and for laying the foundations of new gardens with optimism.

This is the time when addicted gardeners rush, covetous, to their dangerously convenient nurseries, in search of new shrubs and trees. It is prime planting time, when roots may become established before spring. Never mind that we place little bare twigs into carefully prepared holes. We already have their magnificent blooms and desirable foliage in the mind's eye.

I fret that these nonchalant friends have a secret they do not share with me. I only know that the amazing amount of work I seem to need to do in winter determines what my garden will look like for the rest of the year.

It is best to be positive and not mourn the passing of the year's garden. Think how much there will be to enjoy; even as I write, the sunset of the shortest day is staining the charcoal silhouettes of the bare trees with deepest crimson, and the sun descends with defiant bushfire glow.

Those parts of the garden which are resting are enjoyable (not only for absence of labour). There is a peacefulness about turned earth and quiet mulched beds, and one becomes so much more aware of shape and form without the distraction of flowers and foliage. The cascading branches of the weeping silver pear, *Pyrus salicifolia* 'Pendula', lightly dusted with an early frost, and the filigree tracery of the trees' bare branches later against the sky, are visual treasures given only in winter.

This is the time when we should try to study the 'bones' of our gardens – the foundations, undistracted by the massed blooms and foliage of other seasons. Look to see if we have left a solid framework of trees and shrubs to give shelter and privacy. Whether we have enough evergreen, variegated and coloured foliage (especially of reds and golds) to bring warmth to short, half-lit days.

Winter has a chameleon face. How often, caught unawares, have we stepped out to a garden transformed by the brittle fingers of a heavy frost, to find bare branches, gates and fences hung with cobwebs of Etruscan lace? And crunched with tingling feet across paddocks crackling with rime, and across lawns embroidered by bird prints? This old enemy bespangles the garden with exquisite etchings, as though to compensate for the poor plants scorched by his searing breath during mischievous midnight play.

In 1923 Marion Cran wrote, 'I love even the grim fighting hours of deep winter when frost is hammering at the lives of the flowers, and earth withdraws all life to her fastness.'

Without winter we should not see the filigree stencils of frost flowers on the outside windows of the greenhouse, (rejoicing that all inside is safe and warm) or witness the transformation of the blanched skeletons, of old stalky seed pods which have escaped the secateurs, reborn in a new life of gilded silver.

For many of us there will be the snow days, when the cherished and familiar garden disappears, enfolded in a white cocoon. The grey days are replaced with ones of radiant and eerie light, and, drawing the curtains at bedtime, we see a garden made secret by moonlight as pale as the snow it rides. Only the water in our ornamental pools and ponds is untouched by snow.

Made restless by long hours of winter's house arrest, we rebel and, wrapping up warmly, go into the garden searching desperately for signs of life – a few flowers to pick – anything. If we have planned and planted for these grimmer days, our gardener's hearts sing at the sight of carpets of tiny blue *Anemone blanda,* ruffled aconites of varnished gold, and snowdrops – all making pools of colour in the snow like fire in opals. There may be a few early crocus, so delicate, so small, lavender-blue like the tiny china teacups of a doll's teaset I cherished as a child.

We may have planned to beat the winter blues by planting clumps of *Iris unguicularis.* (syn. *I. stylosa*). Searching the grass, we are rewarded by the sight of blooms of a blue to rival the sky of the most brilliant of frosty days in intensity. Perhaps it will be possible to pick, with cold, numbed fingers, a few sprays of wintersweet, *Chimonanthus praecox*, bearing curious flowers which look like exotic golden spiders and smell sweetly of almonds; or of the perfumed multi-flowered heads of *Luculia gratissima* or the old favourite *Viburnum fragrans*.

I find the scented flowers of mid-winter fascinating because they have so few insects to woo at this time. Perhaps Nature has given their sweet fragrance for human beings alone, to make more bearable winter's darker days.

How very much more we appreciate the flowers of winter. They are fewer, and so more precious. We do not take them for granted like those of spring and summer. It is worth having winter purely for being able to pick bunches of violets and the small heads of *Daphne odora leucanthe*, unbelieving of the sweetness of their fragrance. I picked a tiny tussie-mussie of both today, and have them in an antique jug of silver on my desk. They are my jewels of winter.

Such flowers are small and exquisite, treasured for their fragile beauty, but the real ice maidens are the flowers of the *Helleborus* species, the winter rose. I have naturalised them in great drifts, together with 'paper white' narcissi, beneath my trees. They give abundantly of their radiant flowers, which can be picked in luxuriant posies, on the grey days when it seems as though winter will go on forever. I am quite bewitched by the flowers of *Helleborus* 'White Magic', which are spiked with lemon stamens and shimmer with translucent purity when lit by stray sunbeams.

If drama instead of delicacy is what you require for winter-weary corners, the green-white parasol flowers of the Corsican hellebore, *H. argutifolius*, are the ones for you. The blooms, washed with peach as they age, are freely given atop tall stalks with handsome foliage.

For pure versatility in colour and form, the finest hellebores are derived from the *orientalis* species. The flowers now come in delicious dusky reds, blushing pinks, green, primrose, yellow, stunning plums, purples and even slate-blues. Many blooms are beautifully freckled with darker spots. They are the stars of my winter garden, treasured as much for their beauty and generosity as for their bravery in the face of fang-like winds and battering rains.

If you have grown cold with all this talk of frost, snow and storm, plan for an evening of armchair gardening, scented with woodsmoke and warmth. Spend it in an orgy of glossy catalogues. As the old saying goes, 'Faith will never die as long as brightly coloured plant and seed catalogues are printed . . .'. Feast and covet through their pages, and indulge in creating gardens of visual extravaganzas in the mind. The creative hangover next morning will soon be lost in contemplation of the new day, coming to the garden with mystery, concealing its weariness with muslin veils of mist which marry earth and sky, making the paddocks look like a sea without a shore. Little wisps, lit by a spectral sun, wander through the bare branches of the fruit trees and fringe the edges of the ornamental pool.

True, there are the forlorn, the never-ending days in winter when we are imprisoned inside in a ringing cage of rain; when the soil has become a sticky, reddish, brutish, treacly morass which can take hold of a spade and never give it back. But with mud and flood there comes also a sense of security, the sure knowledge that the season, with its eternal wisdom and cycle, unaided by man, is storing the liquid reserves in the earth so that it may survive the thirst of summer months, weary with heat and dust.

Winter is a looking forward, a time of anticipation, the time when we can see with inward vision the blooms which will break from the furry fat buds of the magnolia trees, when we are teased by the growth we cannot see, but know is there, happening in bulb magic beneath the earth. It is a time of waiting, a season hung suspended, until the quickening pulse of spring, waking the Sleeping Beauty garden of winter, brushes aside the gentle reflections of fireside evenings, and sends us scurrying once more to boot and spade.

CHAPTER THIRTY-TWO

PLANTING RAINBOWS
FOR WINTER

One of the questions I am most frequently asked by visitors is, 'What can I plant for winter colour? It would not be difficult to write several chapters about the colourful plants which are available for this purpose, so I must confine myself (with difficulty) to writing about those which are making glowing spots of colour on this cold, wet August day at Valley Homestead.

I find groupings of red, gold and silver most effective for providing warmth, offset by variegated and plain green foliage. Natives are superb for this and have the added bonus of being hardy and requiring little attention.

Of the evergreen shrubs, the tough coprosmas provide most attractive variegated foliage. *Coprosma*. 'Marble King' and *C.* 'Marble Queen' have cream leaves which look as though someone has sprayed tiny speckles of green paint on them, giving a marbled effect. *C. repens* 'Variegata' rejoices in rounded leaves with an irregular central zone of deep green, broadly margined with deep yellow, which look as though they have been polished. This coprosma is not prostrate as the name suggests but grows to a handsome shrub and clips well. *C. robusta* 'Variegata' and *C. r.* 'Williamsii' I use as great lighteners of shaded or darker corners, where they do well. Both have prettily variegated leaves of creamy whites and greens. They are not quite as robust as the other coprosmas but, given a little shelter, will thrive. *C. r.* 'Williamsii' has slender stems, giving a graceful and pendulous effect.

C. repens 'Painter's Palette' is a gem, with wonderful shiny foliage of bronzy sunset-pinks and olive-greens. No winter garden can manage without this one. *C.* 'Pink Splendour' is also great for softer pink tones.

Whenever I visit Europe I am always delighted to see how highly prized our *Phormium* – flaxes – and cabbage trees (*Cordyline*) are for landscaping. But their price is astonishing, and I cannot believe our good fortune that they are our natives, and that we can choose from a wonderful selection for a reasonable price. My favourites have already been described in chapter seventeen.

As the perfect contrast to the coloured phormium gang, I should hate to be without our handsome native *Astelia chathamica*, which has silver swords for leaves. This is a dramatic plant for areas where bold statements are required; its leaves glisten with quicksilver after a shower of rain.

Conifers with their varied forms make excellent companions for the flaxes and provide further colour tones. A particular favourite with a name it does not deserve is *Chaemacyparis pisifera* 'Filifera Aurea'. This is a pretty dwarf conifer with drooping, thread-like yellow foliage, which gives a softly flowing effect, especially among more upright forms such the pencil pine, *Cupressus* 'Swanes Golden'. I have a weakness also for the dwarf conifer *Thuya occidentalis* 'Rheingold'. It has almost feathery foliage which turns to a glowing bronze in winter. *Coleonema* 'Sunset Gold' will give clear yellow tones, and looks especially effective interplanted with blue grasses such as *Festuca ovina* 'Glauca'.

For further gilding of the garden with gold to cheer grey days, the *Euonymus* shrubs are excellent. *E. japonicus* 'Aureomarginatus', the golden Japanese laurel, has glossy oval leaves, heavily margined with gold. Naturally narrow, erect and compact in growth, it may be clipped to any desired shape. *E. japonicus* 'Ovatus Aureus' is the dwarf golden laurel, which comes bursting with sunshine. It is a delightful, low-growing compact form with golden yellow foliage, lightly shaded with soft green.

Pseudopanax 'Gold Splash', another native, gives warm buttery splashes of gold on a handsome shrub with deeply lobed, five-fingered leaves. This shrub will grow to a height of about two metres but tolerates clipping well. It provides excellent form as a landscaping plant.

Helichrysum petiolare 'Limelight' is a densely petalled trailing or climbing plant with clear lime-green foliage which lightens the drabbest corners. It clips well if a mound effect is desired.

After the sunshiny golds, we need glowing reds for warmth on gold days. Many of the red-toned foliage shrubs I have used in the terraces around the water gardens and on the drive (see chapters seventeen and twenty-two), and will provide the necessary winter warmth.

As a foil to the reds and golds, plain grey foliage which still looks good without the sun's heat may be provided by *Helichrysum petiolare*, a densely foliaged climbing or sprawling plant which has leaves of soft silver, by *Santolina* (cotton lavender), or by *Artemisia arborescens*, with aromatic foliage. All tolerate well clipping to any desired size.

A shrub which is different and looks good at any time of the year is *Mahonia lomariifolia* (Chinese holly grape). It is invaluable for winter colour and interest, and as a dramatic landscaping plant. Its large evergreen leaves are divided into spiny leaflets, 7–10 centimetres long, arranged symmetrically along both sides of the midrib. They are attached directly in a horizontal plane, arranged near the tips of each stem. In winter, huge clusters of tiny yellow bell-shaped flowers appear, followed by gorgeous powdery blue and purple berries, which the birds adore.

Of the winter-flowering shrubs, two of the best come from China: witch hazel *Hamamelis mollis*) and wintersweet (*Chimonanthus praecox*). The former has curious spidery golden yellow flowers, which have an almond fragrance and appear on bare branches. The branches themselves are angular, forming an attractive oriental zig-zag pattern. Wintersweet has yellow flowers splashed with purple, and surprises one by smelling of violets.

Immediately outside the back door I have planted the incomparable *Daphne odora* 'Leucanthe', and as I pass I can pick one of the small multi-flowered pinkish heads, knowing that in a tiny vase it will scent practically a whole room.

An indulgence against my studio wall has been the planting of winter-blooming *Luculia gratissima* 'Early Dawn', which is as generous with its soft-pink blooms as with its sweet scent. Together with these excellent shrubs, which give both flowers and perfume to the winter garden, who could forget the *Viburnum* species? The old favourites *V.* x *burkwoodii* or *V. fragrans* are hard to beat, but an interesting new cultivar is *V. carlesii* 'Aurora', which has greyish leaves, pink buds, strongly perfumed flowers and gives a good red autumn colour – a shrub of immense virtue.

We could not fail to include some camellias in the winter garden – the sasanquas for early blooming, and the bright heads of the hybrids to see us through the season. There are a great many from which to choose, from small patio or container species to those suitable for hedging, and the shrub bushes with upright or spreading form. I have a passion for the sumptuous warming black-reds and vibrant pinks of 'Night Rider', 'Dr Clifford Parkes', 'Guilio Nuccio', 'Valentine's Day', 'Donation' and 'Purple Gown'.

Leucadendrons are my other great standy for almost all-year-round colour, especially the old favourites *L.* 'Safari Sunset' and

L. 'Laureolum'. The former bears large bracts of intense coral-reds and the latter of dazzling chrome-yellow – winter cheer for even the gloomiest day. Another long-lasting splash of gold is provided by *Reinwardtia indica*, from the mountains of India, a small bush which bears bell-shaped blooms of buttery yellow for many weeks in the middle of the year.

For flowers to pick all winter, the hellebore species from the Northern Hemisphere – where they are known as 'winter roses' – are gems. There are many different species, of which the most hardy is *Helleborus orientalis*. The colours range from pure whites through shades of pink to dusky crimson-purple. They look best naturalised in large clumps under trees, and on those bleak grey days when one prowls around the garden looking for something – anything – to pick, they will be blooming with such abundance that it will be possible to pick enough for a luxurious vase fall.

A list of smaller flowers to fold in among the winter shrubs might include the *Primula* species, especially the dainty little *P. malacoides*, which seeds itself happily everywhere and seems to look right wherever it springs up, as do the pansy and viola species. A recent introduction of cold-hardy pansies hybridised for winter blooming is the 'Romeo and Juliet' mixture.

Velvety wallflowers, *Cheiranthus*, antirrhinum, the bright cineraria daisy flowers, and linarias will bloom in all but the harshest of conditions. The selection of winter-flowering bulbs is enormous, and would fill a chapter on its own. Take the easy option – a bulb catalogue of dazzling colour, a log on the fire, your favourite armchair, and a glass of wine. In your mind's eye plant colour for next winter – ixias, spraxis, crocus, tulips, daffodils, jonquils, narcissus, hyacinth, freesias . . . the choice and the colours are yours.

CHAPTER THIRTY-THREE

AN ORCHARD GARDEN
FOR VALLEY HOMESTEAD

I have been to England in April. I have trodden damp and mossy woods full of bluebells, travelled along narrow, winding country lanes smothered in primroses in Devon and Cornwall. I have laughed at showers of confetti tossed from cherry trees in ancient thatched villages in Hampshire. I have seen the Kentish countryside folded with clusters of old red-brick oast-houses wearing witches' hats, where hops once dried. English orchards, with blossoms in their hair and wildflowers at their feet, have sent me home enchanted.

And I have been to Sissinghurst! Garden walls of ancient yew or centuries-old red brick, castle towers, leaded windows, pleached lime walks, or moated gardens I cannot have, but the orchard garden behind my eyes, full of wildflowers and bulbs, shall be mine, growing well in the kind Northland climate.

I cannot have the ancient beauty of the knotted and gnarled trunks of the fruit trees in Vita Sackville-West's orchard, which have already outlived a generation. But I may possess the knowledge that the trees I shall shortly plant will, one day, give the same sense of age and permanence to those who walk in my garden after me, and in whose future I can have no part but this.

In just a few years, from the beginning of the planting of my wild garden, I will be able to sit beneath my young trees, and share the scent of spring and the harvest of autumn with them. I will plant my orchard garden with apple trees bearing flowers of pink and white porcelain, cherries foaming great froths of blossoms of carmines and purest whites. I will plant a fig, peaches and nectarines, so that my family may experience the sensuous delight of picking and eating sun-warmed fruit straight from the tree. I must have a pear tree, of ancient French lineage, I think, 'Beurre Bosc' perhaps. And in among the sharp scent of the citrus I will plant an apricot, 'Sundrop', for its fruit with pinkish blush.

Beneath the trees, in grassy cradle, I will plant small, fragrant seas of narcissi with names such as 'Dove Wings' and 'Silver Chimes'. I will plant great clumps of golden cowslips and pale lemon primroses, fragile in morning dews. There shall be small wild tulips in soft colours, tiny scillas of pinks, whites and blues – *Scilla sibirica* 'Spring Beauty' and *S. hispanica*, the Spanish bluebell. There shall be whole azure carpets of English bluebells (*Scilla non-scripta*) for my grandchildren's feet.

In gorgeous abundance, in the fruit trees' shade, I will plant the fascinating freckled and spotted snake's head fritillary, *Fritillaria meleagris*, and lavender *F. pyrenaica* and *F. persica*, modestly nodding their bell heads, whispering the names of exotic, faraway countries to the spring breezes.

This visual extravaganza behind my eyes is not yet complete. I must have tender drifts of fragile blue and white *Anemone blanda* and *A. apenina* for my orchard woodland. There must be clumps of wild crocuses of cream, feathered royal-purple on the outside, and of sulphur-yellows and golds. They shall be threaded through with the intense blue spikes of the grape hyacinth, *Muscari*. The air in my orchard garden shall be rich with the scent of wild violets – *V. odorata*, with heart-shaped leaves, enchanting little pink *V.* 'Coeur d'Alsace' and *V. labradorica* 'Purpurea', with dark purple leaves and flowers of tenderest blue.

No uncouth voice of lawnmower shall ever approach the dream garden. Long and luxuriant the grass shall grow, threaded through, tumbled and tinted with my wild, free-flowering treasures.

When I am an old, old woman with long grey moustaches, baggy, garden-weathered cardigans, stout boots and a cane, like Josephine Nuese in her Garden of Primroses, I shall kneel with creaking knees and pick myself tussie-mussies of scented violets, primroses and fragile anemones. I will place them in my lap and, resting in an old chair, I will doze in the sun and dream of when I was fit and strong and planted my orchard garden.

CHAPTER THIRTY-FOUR

THE EDIBLE
GARDEN

When Brian installed the water-storage tank for the irrigation system, he placed it in a discreet corner of the paddock adjacent to the orchard garden. I bethought me that the sunny corner was the perfect spot for a small vege plot. Before he fenced it off from the cattle, I whipped in some punnets of spring veges. On the day he and Jim brought in their fencing materials and he roared, 'What's all this?' I muttered about how well the vege plants were growing, and of vast savings on the home-economy front. 'Bloody woman's been at it again, Jim,' said Brian, rolled his eyes heavenwards and moved the fencing lines out a bit further.

I think vege plots, or *le jardin potager*, the kitchen and cook's garden, should be as beautiful as any other part of the garden, and once my corner had been legitimised, I had the greatest fun trying to make it so. It is entered through a simple archway flanked by a pair of silvery cypresses – *Chamaecyparis lawsoniana* 'Fletcheri', Gertrude Jekyll's 'pudding trees'. The archway is clothed with the soft apricot-gold climbing rose 'Lady Hillingdon', through which blue sweetpeas scramble to scent my hours of labour.

I laid pathways of old red bricks (lots more visits to the

demolition yard, aching back and creaking knees!) to an Elizabethan design. The pathways radiate from a central circular bed, where *Rosa gallica officinalis*, the apothecary's rose, now sits, underplanted with the catmint *Nepeta faassenii*. This rose of ancient lineage has been used since medieval times for culinary, medicinal and toiletry preparations. It is valued today for its hardiness and the beauty of its semi-double, richly fragrant flowers. The rose has attractive dark green leaves and an erect bushy growth habit.

In this small garden I play with favourite herbs: the wonderfully pungent curry plant, *Helichrysum angustifolium*, which is delicious in hard-boiled-egg mixtures as well as savoury dishes; aromatic rosemary; the dark rosy purple and pretty tri-coloured green, cream and mauve sages. I planted handsome bronze fennel, lots of different chives with nodding lavender pom-pom heads, silvery soft cotton lavender, *Santolina neapolitana*, and many others which take my fancy – and that of the bees.

I made a simple seat next to the scented herb garden. An ancient weathered piece of totara fencepost 'borrowed' from Brian's 'might come in useful pile', set across leftover bricks at either end, made the most pleasant of resting places.

Four fat leeks, a creamy cauliflower head, a pretty red winter lettuce, and a generous bunch of herbs – in they go into my 'filling' basket. We have gathered many a meal together, this old friend and I. Reaping from one harvest today, we have sown another. How enjoyable it was on this late September day, putting in the new season's tomato plants, conjuring up images of juicy red fruit on crisp beds of summer salads. All gardeners are optimists and cunning. To lessen the shock of the cold wet soil for the delicate seedlings, I made them warm overcoats of two-litre polythene milk bottles with the bottoms cut off. These work well for any small new plants, protecting them from inclement weather. They keep away slugs and snails also, so that one does not have to use expensive toxic pellets.

In front of the tomatoes I planted a row of pea seedlings already sprouting silvery, clinging tendrils. When grown, the peas, together with the tasty cocktail tomatoes ('Sun Cherry') bring on dreadful attacks of gluttony. I have been known to start at one end of a row of new peas and, working my way along, leave a trail of discarded pods behind me. Only guilty thoughts of depriving Brian of the joy of their sweet tenderness on his plate restrains me. As for the rows of strawberries put in under the peas, small white flowers already forming, it takes a wily bird to beat me to the plump red berries . . .

As I weed among the broad beans, I wonder if the bees, droning ecstatically in the hearts of their black-and-white flowers, know they are safe from toxic spray. I am paranoic about organically grown veges and fruit, thus the joy of having a working lunch in the edible gardens at any time. I grow enough for the bugs and me and mine, and use only organic sprays when necessary. It wasn't always so. When, as a novice gardener, I began making the gardens six years ago, I would drench my plants with any toxic chemical the helpful garden-centre staff would sell me. Night after night, as I read my 'how-to' gardening books, lurid and highly graphic pictures would leap from the page at me, of pests and diseases grotesque enough to strike terror into the amateur's heart. Their very names smacked of foul decay – rot, corky scab, wilt, blight, fungus, black spot, club root, rust, leaf curl, botrytis, and mildews – which had the bonus of manifesting themselves in several different varieties.

As though this weren't enough, there followed lists of disgusting pests whose destructive capabilities were apparently legendary; black, green and white flies, mealy bugs, thrips, leafhoppers, white butterflies, caterpillars, green and bronze 'stinky beetles', red spider mite, scale insects, codling moth –

the ghastly list made slugs and snails seem like desirable domestic pets.

I used to go to bed envisioning whole armies of these grotesque vampirish beasts invading my new gardens, and inflicting decimating plagues of biblical proportions.

I bought a backpack and enough toxic chemicals to annihilate plant life from several acres, and dispensed death vengefully whenever I saw a few aphids. Then a friend, much older and wiser in the ways of gardening than I, seeing me striding about goggled, hooded, booted and suited like a demented astronaut, asked me to stop and think about what I was doing.

I vacillated uneasily between the use of diabolical chemicals and the dread of plant decimation by gruesome pests and diseases. I began to read about an organic approach to gardening and became consumed with guilt about the beneficial and necessary insects which had fallen pray to my unnecessary spray-gun. I have never used toxic chemicals in the garden since; I still have my share of unpleasant insectiferous pests, mildews, black spot, fungus, etc., but I still had all these in abundance in the days when I was spraying death from the air with reckless abandon.

My favourite, highly effective homemade spray comes from pyrethrum – *Chrysanthemum cinerariifolium*. This plant is often referred to as the 'insect plant' because its flowers make the safest of all organic insecticides. The white, yellow-centred daisies contain pyrethrins, which act directly on the nervous systems of insects such as aphids, mites and caterpillars. Pyrethrins are harmless to other plants, animal and human life.

Chrysanthemum cinerariifolium has serrated grey foliage and thrives in any sunny, well-drained area of the vege garden. To make the spray, mix about twenty millilitres, or one tablespoon, of fresh crushed flowers with a little alcohol to release the pyrethrins. (The flower can be dried and stored for use at other times of the year.) Place the ground mixture into two litres of hot water and add a squirt of dishwashing detergent to make the aphids unhappy and aid the spray's stickability. Allow to stand, and strain when cool.

To make insect-repellent garlic spray, which may be added to the pyrethrum, take a whole bulb of garlic, peel and crush the individual cloves, bring them to the boil in half a litre of water, simmer for a few minutes until the garlic is soft, then cool and strain it. Obviously the more cloves one uses, the more repellent the brew. Remember not to spray your roses just before a coachload of visitors is due!

For busy gardeners who do not have time to make their own spray, there are several excellent pyrethrum- and garlic-based organic sprays available at garden centres. These will take care of the bugs, and can safely be mixed with organic copper and sulphur mixtures so that one may have both pesticide and fungicide in one preparation.

When I am making my spray I am reminded of an enthusiastic old gentleman who pressed upon me a recipe for an organic spray involving the collection of the beastly green sap-sucking beetles which dine on the veges and roses. The beasts are dropped into a bowl of soapy water to kill them, then the awful mixture is popped into the kitchen whizz – yuk! (Does his wife know?) The result is an evil-smelling green goo which must stand, be strained and then diluted. The dear gentleman told me it was the most effective organic spray he had ever found and had rid his garden of plagues of the dread green beetle. However, I have to admit to having passed on this one and stuck to the manufacture of my more wholesome flowerhead and garlic sprays.

The bugs catered for, I look to means of deterring the birds, and the rabbits which frolic in from the paddocks to feast on the tender new broccoli and lettuces. Indulging in a grand tantrum after one of their particularly vicious raids, I put up a scarecrow

— or scareperson. He/she is only partially effective — the birds roost along the person's arms and the rabbits hide under flapping overcoat tails — all eyeing up which juicy plant they will pick off next.

Studying the scareperson on a warm September morning, it occurred to me that his/her total lack of taste in clothing was the reason for the inefficiency in scaring away the raiders. I resolved to call in at the 'op shop' on my next trip to town and treat the person to a whole new outfit for spring, in the brightest and best bird- and rabbit-scaring colours available.

For drama in the edible garden, I indulge in a pair of globe artichoke plants, *Cynara scolymus*. Their huge spiky grey felted leaves give a magnificent architectural effect, and their large globose heads, like giant thistles, if not eaten, are wonderful for dried floral arrangements.

Perhaps my most favourite part of the vege garden, after the herb area, is the border. I have combined the bright lime-green foliage of feverfew, *Chrysanthemum parthenium aureum,* with the stunning intense blue flower spikes of the English lavender 'Hidcote', and the dark purple leaves of opal basil, *Ocimum basilicum*. The basil and feverfew are good companion plants for keeping away troublesome insects, too, as are marigolds, garlic, chives, nasturtium, phacelia and yarrow. Beneficial insects, such as the hoverfly and the ladybird, which love to dine on aphids, are attracted in great numbers to the latter.

Taking my picking basket into the herb and vege garden and filling it is a joy that is never diminished, like the turning of the seasons, no matter how many times the process is repeated. But too much leaning on the spade and meditating means less to put in the harvest basket.

CHAPTER THIRTY-FIVE

FADS AND FASHION IN THE HERB GARDEN

Recently, through bad planning, just before guests were due to arrive for supper, I found myself frantically scrabbling in the vege garden between giant broccoli and globe artichoke leaves for a handful of herbs, dressed in a white silk suit. The ruination of my (rare) sartorial elegance made me resolve to create an easily accessible and separate herb garden.

I withdrew two books from the library, the first a book on trendy herb-garden design and the second on the history of the herb garden. The latter made excellent reading, and taking a brief step back in history, I learned that in medieval days, roughly from the years 600 to 1500, the growing of herbs in Europe was done in a very utilitarian manner by monks. Every monastery had a *herbularis* or physic garden, which was composed of oblong beds intersected by paths. The herbs needed for treating the sick were placed near the infirmary door and those for culinary purposes near the kitchen. Sweet-smelling herbs and flowers, gall or wormwood, were used for strewing on the floor to 'dispelle ye bad odoures', to 'destroy fleas' or for 'cleansing ye aire of pestilence and ye plague' (medieval pollution?). Like those for decoration of home and church, these were grown in the cloister garth.

In those days the mistress of every castle surrounded by a

moat was always expected to be an expert at growing herbs. This she did in the only space available to her within the castle courtyards or, in the case of castles which were ringed by double walls instead of a moat, within gardens between the walls. Castles and monasteries always had a stillroom near the kitchen, and the monks would train m'lady in the use of herbs for medicinal and culinary purposes.

In the stillroom she would supervise the compounding of healing ointments, medicines, sweet oils and waters, pomanders to disguise body odours, and potpourris – arts in which she was expected to be proficient. Not only did her knight returning in tarnished armour, the worse for wear from his battles, tournaments or hunting, look to her for nursing aid, but she was also responsible for the health and wellbeing of everyone else within the castle walls – a busy lady.

Leaving m'lady to her ancient arts, I studied the book on 'trendy' designs for herb gardens. I have before me a delightful if unusual, plan for a herb rockery. It is beautifully drawn and coloured in, and everything planted therein is growing lustily, behaving beautifully and blooming at the same time. Angelica, which grows huge and requires shade and damp feet, grows to a modest sixty centimetres in the middle of heat-loving thymes, rosemary and sages. Tall bronze fennel, which likes to flaunt its feathery plumes above my head, nestles coyly, short and squat, in a small corner. Root-invasive mints sit obediently in the neat space allotted them and would obviously not dream of sending out stealthy runners to invade everybody else's space.

You name it, it is all there in a picture to enthrall the naïve beginner. Regrettably, no instructions are forthcoming regarding the requirements and habit of each plant, or of their size and when full grown. It would appear that all one has to do is shove the herbs into any soil showing between the rocks, and the fairies at the bottom of the garden will do the rest.

The next design is for a herb garden indoors. This incorporates herbs growing in tiny pots, perched on narrow shelves fitted across the kitchen windows. What happens when one needs to open them, or when a recipe calls for more than one leaf of mint or a single sprig of parsley not revealed. I am encouraged, though, as the page ends with a sentence suggesting that herbs can be grown in pots outside the kitchen door.

I turn over for further instruction, but it seems that potted herbs in so practical a place are obviously not trendy, and far too mundane an idea for further comment. There are, instead, delightful designs for large, formal buxus-bordered overseas knot gardens overflowing with rare herbs, which have been established for centuries. The author suggests that most suburban dwellers with homes built on small plots 'could easily find a small corner to give one a go'. I am aghast. While most of us who live in rural areas could, if we wish, 'lean' on paddock fences to indulge in herb gardens of such size and elegance, I cannot imagine how any of my friends in town could incorporate miniatures of such grandiose designs in their plots, or what on earth they would look like if they did.

The author waxes eloquent on herb wheels and ladders. For these designs, one must collect the antique wagon wheels and wooden ladders which are lying around all over town. The prettily coloured pictures again show a selection of herbs of totally different growth habits and requirements, all sitting obediently in the confines of their trendy containers. I know that there is not going to be a picture overleaf of the plants which have quickly outgrown their fashionable spoke and rung confines, ending up in a sprawling, unsightly, jumbled mass.

The next design has a horrible fascination. It would, I admit, be possible to lay out a herb garden hedged with box in the shape of a huge butterfly, if the author helped with a list of carefully selected plants for their low growth habits, and just mentioned the back-breaking attention with clippers it would constantly require.

There are designs for herb gardens in the shape of diamonds, hearts and clubs (yuk); in lozenges, triangles, in old boots, prams, wheelbarrows and even in a toilet bowl. I am bemused when, turning back to the introduction of the book, I find the author states that the designs are for 'Gardeners wanting to get back to the simple, natural way of herb gardening'. I am puzzled that we are instructed to do so in such an erroneous, impractical and highly stylised manner.

The size and shape of a herb garden, and the plants one can grow in it, will be governed by the quality of soil, and the shape and aspect of one's overall garden. For most of us, a sunny, well-drained area adjacent to the vege garden, or a corner of the house or patio allotted to pots, will house all the herbs we use most frequently. The taller growers – borage, angelica and fennel – can soar away happily at the back, while parsley, chives, garlic, lemon verbena, etc., comfortably occupy mid positions, and the real sun-worshippers – rosemary, sages, thymes and oreganos – roast themselves along the front. I still recommend the potting of the mints because of their invasive root systems, wherever the herb garden might be.

The 'trendy' book was returned to the shelf, and I decided on a simple potted *herbularis*, adjacent to the vege garden for quick and easy picking, and where watering would be taken care of by the resident sprinkler. I used old bricks in raised layers, left over from making paths in the vege garden, to form a circle. I planted favourite herbs in terracotta pots of varying sizes, depending on the growth requirements of the plants, and used plenty of 'liquid rain' crystals. (Was there a life before 'Crystal Rain'?) Terracotta pots can be expensive in garden centres, but large chain stores often have them on special offer, and secondhand bricks, paving stones and tiles can also be bought for reasonable prices in demolition yards, or as 'seconds' from builder's merchants.

When completed, the simple circular herb garden in pots, on its raised-brick base, has made a quickly accessible, practical and attractive focal-point adjacent to the vege garden and, happily, spells the end of playing 'hunt the parsley' in party gear.

A HERB FOR
ALL SEASONS

Every Friday morning, come rain, hail, frost or sun, Miss Margie Maddren, recipient of the QSM for conservation work, sits behind her stall in front of the Ladies' Gardening Club in Whangarei, selling fund-raising plants and dispensing advice from the depths of a great knowledge of native plants and other species.

Margie, born in 1922, cannot get about too easily now. Though a double hip-replacement last year freed her from some degree of pain, she still has problems with mobility. In spite of this, an indomitable spirit ensures that she may be found sitting for many hours each day in front of her garage, potting up hundreds of donated cuttings. It is with the proceeds from the sale of the rooted plants that the Whangarei Native Bird and Forest Protection Society, of which Margie has been president for over two-and-a-half decades, has funded major conservation projects in Northland for as many years.

I had the good fortune to meet Margie about six years ago, when I was beginning the gardens at Valley Homestead on a very limited budget. At this stage, new to New Zealand, I would take her plants for identification – sometimes prime specimens from the noxious weed patches I had been nurturing, waiting for them to burst into exotic Antipodean bloom: onion weed, wild ginger, oxalis with its prettily shaped leaves . . .

Taking a keen interest in my 'gorse to gardens' project, Margie always pointed out little pots on her stall containing something 'which would do well at your place'. Knowing that one of my first priorities was to build up a stock of potted herbs, one morning she said, 'Here, this is especially for you. This is allherb.'

I was intrigued by the deliciously strong fragrance of the plant's thick, pale-green, fleshy leaves, which almost resembled those of a succulent. They grow opposite each other on short, individual pinkish stalks, from a central root. They are also hairy and heavily veined underneath, and the older leaves have a pinkish line around their frilly edges. Small new leaves grow in pairs in the axils of the larger leaves, which bear insignificant pale pink flowers with a fused lower lip on their tips in late summer to autumn. The plant's enticing smell seemed a combination or oregano, camphor, sage, thyme and citrus, all rolled into one.

This combination of flavours and scents probably explains why I subsequently had such trouble tracking down its history and origin. I thumbed through the indexes of dozens of learned tomes, before Margie lent me one of her many special reference books. The plant appeared in this as a member of the *Coleus* family, under no less than ten names – thus my extreme difficulties with indexing. Gertrude B. Foster, writing in *The Herb Grower*, vol. XXV, 3, 1972, comments: 'Five Seasons Herb – *Coleus amboinicus* syn. *Coleus aromaticus*. . . . Certainly the oregano scent and flavour are strong and the texture of the foliage and stems are quite different from the ornamental *Coleus* used for summer bedding plants . . . '.

The herb comes from the island of Amboin in the East Indies and was taken to Europe by Spanish explorers, which would explain its names Spanish thyme or Spanish sage. The herb's most common name appears to be five seasons herb or allherb, followed by: Indian borage, Puerto Rican oregano, Puerto Rican thyme, country borage, three-in-one and five-in-one. It is used extensively in the West Indies, the Pacific Islands and South-East Asia. It has been in New Zealand for less than a decade, and deserves to become much more widely known for its powerful aromatic seasoning for culinary purposes.

Margie and I found the herb propagated easily from cuttings, but only under very warm conditions. It does well in hot summers, given free-draining soil, and in a sheltered place will spread to make a low, sprawling clump of handsome, aromatic leaves. It grows very well in pots, and because it is a tropical plant we found it was essential to take cuttings in late summer and overwinter them indoors on a draught-free sunny window sill or in a glasshouse. The herb requires little watering during the winter months.

The leaves of *Coleus amboinicus* are excellent used in stuffings for chicken and pork, in stews, dumplings, soups, casseroles and salads, on pizzas or in any food where a strong aromatic herb flavouring is required. The leaves are best lightly chopped to release their powerful flavouring.

You may call it what you will. For me it will always be 'Margie's herb', but once it is part of your collection, you will wonder how you managed without this versatile five seasons, five flavours gem of the herb garden.

CHAPTER THIRTY-SEVEN

THE SPADE'S
FULL CIRCLE

Six years ago when I began the brutal toil of creating a garden from bare paddocks, nothing could have been further from my mind than ending up with one which would be open to the public. At this time, 'open gardens' were usually large and well known nationwide. Welcoming paying guests into private gardens, regardless of size or design, and of their use for fundraising and charity events, was a concept which was only just beginning to emerge. It is now a booming movement which has led to a 'Great Garden Revival'. 'Garden safaries', parties and festivals have become popular leisure activities and lucrative fundraisers, and are turning us into a nation of keen, skilled and knowledgeable gardeners.

'Going public' has probably been the steepest learning curve I have embarked upon. It began with a phone call from a lady who said she had heard I was making some interesting gardens, and requested permission to bring a group of terminally ill cancer patients to walk in them. I replied that I would be honoured and delighted. This event somehow snowballed, and before I knew it, the volume of visitors was growing with the garden.

As the garden matured, and visitor numbers continued to spiral, the dilemma of whether to charge an admission fee inevitably arose. I decided I would prefer an 'admission by donation' approach, the proceeds going to a major charity. Sadly, this idea never really worked; even after several coachloads of visitors, there would scarcely be a few dollars in the collection box. One evening, after a large, well-funded group left, it contained sixty cents. That same evening an unnamed rose cutting from the roadside bloomed, and we promptly called it 'Sixty Cents'.

At this stage, also, I knew I would have to buy a larger, more powerful lawnmower and pay for a couple of hours' help with mowing each week. Balancing the time spent showing visitors around and answering their questions with the amount of maintenance required to keep the garden to a standard acceptable to the public was becoming increasingly difficult. Finally an admission fee was set, and I had truly 'gone public'.

Another hurdle on the economic front, at this point, is consideration of the necessity for the provision of toilet facilities. Confidence in a steady flow of visitors during the time the garden is open is required to justify the expense of building an exterior lavatory. The alternative is a coachload of visitors or total strangers, no matter how nice they might be, needing to invade the privacy of your home and family because they are desperate for the toilet.

From a strictly economic point of view, in proportion to the time and labour involved, opening your garden to paying guests will never make a second income, but it will pay for a few hours help with maintenance each week, and leave a little extra to spare – which goes straight back into the garden, of course.

'Going public' means becoming hopelessly addicted to the weather forecast and living in a state of constant neurosis about what the weather is, or is not, going to do. Of knowing that it is a forgone conclusion that wind and rain will devastate the garden into which you have put hours of hard labour for a large charity event. If it does not pour torrents and blow gales the day before (when the lawns have to be mown, come hell or high water – literally), it will certainly do so on the day. It is equally certain that the day after will be calm, dry and, of course, sunny. This agonised obsession with the vagaries of the weather can lead to alcohol dependency, or the need for counselling.

'Going public' means never being able to put off until tomorrow what needs to be done today – even if it entails weeding half-dead with flu, or mowing until midnight. Visitors can have quite high expectations, and have 365-degree panoramic vision as far as sickly plants, unpruned shrubs or weeds are concerned. They do not want to see a bed of roses desperately in need of dead-heading. (This is a relaxing chore by moonlight.)

It means imposing the rigorous discipline upon oneself to allow enough time to complete all the garden chores which need doing before visitor arrival time, with a little time left to spare. Guests coming from a distance often arrive early, and I learned the 'time to spare' rule quickly after being obliged to greet a coachload of beautifully turned-out visitors while myself covered in mud from head to toe, soaking wet, with chattering teeth and squelching shoes. I had slipped and fallen into the pond adjacent to the bog garden, in which I had decided I had enough time for a quick blitz before the visitors arrived. Nor should guests be greeted by a grass-stained wild woman, with perspiration dripping off the end of her nose, because she has left the mowing until the last moment and the temperature has soared to thirty degrees by lunchtime.

The fact that there is no one else to muck out the pig-pen but you does not excuse racing up to visitors dishevelled and malodorous. It is a good idea to practise making split-second changes of clothing. The mud and manure are acceptable (just) if concealed beneath clean jeans and shirt, and not too smelly. Hurtling out of the bedroom towards the front door and strolling casually out with a calm, welcoming smile also needs practice. A hot and harassed hostess does not make for relaxed, tranquil garden guests.

'Going public' means learning to be satisifed with the garden as it is, at *present*, and to bite off one's tongue rather than say, 'You should have seen the delphiniums last week' or, 'Of course, the dahlias will be fantastic in a fortnight's time.' It means schooling oneself never to make excuses for the garden – too hot, too dry, too wet, too cold, too windy, too frosty, etc., etc. – even if it does look as though a typhoon passed your way in the night, and every rose in the garden is a sodden, mildewed heap. The visitors are only interested in what they see in the garden and how it looks *now*.

One learns quickly that, as with any group of people, ninety per cent are wholly delightful, but there will always be the minority who will make you foam at the mouth. Garden visitors are no exception. There is the fierce old lady who will dig up an expensive foxglove bought from a catalogue, tell you, 'It's only a wild thing' and throw it at your feet when asked, politely, for its return. There are also a few young mums who arrive with a carload of children and tell them 'to go and play', knowing we have two unfenced pools. And it is not easy explaining to one's husband, at the end of the day, why the expensive cover of an exterior spa pool is in tatters because it has been used as a trampoline by unsupervised children.

Then there are the groups who take a fancy to a cherished plant and all take 'just a little cutting' or a fistful of seedheads. There is the visitor who will stride around the garden demanding why you haven't labels on *everything*, and the one who will, in front of all the other guests, triumphantly present a weed so huge one has mistaken it for a shrub. The guests, with notebook in hand, who pin you in a corner while other visitors require attention, wanting you to design and plant an instant garden on paper for them, are surprisingly common. These very few less-pleasant visitors give one the best lesson possible on how to be a welcome guest in other people's gardens.

One learns to cope with remarks such as 'Of course, in a cottage-garden situation like yours, you just bung everything in, and it takes care of itself.' The vision of the impenetrable jungle it would become overnight, without constant care and attention, must be allowed to flit silently through one's head. Jaw-clenching is mandatory when a visitor, having studied your treasured collection of silver plants with gratifying thoroughness, announces, 'It will look quite pretty when you get some colour in there.'

It is best to be struck dumb after conversations which go like this:

Guest (accusingly), 'You must spend all day, every day, in the garden.'

Me, 'No, I'm afraid not. My husband is in town all week. I run the farm and gardens with minimal help, try to do voluntary work for conservation and charity, write a little, run my home . . .'

Guest, 'But do you *work*?'

If you can manage to squash in a degree-course in horticulture, garden landscaping, spraying programmes and general garden management (in your spare time), this will be a help. Above all, 'going public' means learning to listen. To listen and try to learn from guests expounding personal gardening philosophies which are in antithesis to one's own. To listen to detailed descriptions of every nook, cranny and plant therein of someone else's garden, of their best begonias, or the splendour of their own perennial border while they are critically eyeing yours. It means learning to listen to guests without once saying, 'I', 'Me', or 'Mine'. This is a hard lesson.

'Going Public' is not without pitfalls, but the satisfaction of knowing that sharing one's garden is giving others pleasure, raising funds and making a positive contribution to the community far outweighs the negative aspects. Above all, an 'open garden' brings through the gate hordes of delightful, knowledgeable gardeners whose passion is your passion and whose pleasure is your pleasure. But hang on to your sense of humour, and remember that old Chinese proverb – 'All gardeners know better than other gardeners.'

NOT AN EPILOGUE
BUT A PROLOGUE

This is a story which can have no ending for, like the garden which is its *raison d'être*, I cannot perceive either as finished, no do I wish either completed in the literal sense of the word. As I attempt to bring the story of the creation of this garden to some sort of 'finis', outside my studio window the winter breeze causes a head of *Luculia gratissima* to tap its massed florets of pink and white against the pane. Hunched over the word processor, I try to convey to electronic memory what the garden at Valley Homestead means to me, but through the open door the garden comes into the room; the scent of the *Luculia* and the brilliant jewels of sound from the throat of a thrush distract me in my struggle for appropriate words.

I see that the camellia buds are swollen with promise, and I know that I shall not be able to write 'finis', and draw a line, for soon I shall be seeking to capture their essence in snare of words, as an artist would endeavour to capture their image with his brush. We both seek to share and communicate with others our joy in the beauty and colour we know they will bring to winter days.

If I write an epilogue, I suspect it will merely become a prologue. Periodically I get on a Boeing 747, span continents and time zones, change worlds in hours, and yet I do not leave the garden behind me. When I am rushing about in the noisy hearts of the great cities, I know that if I close my eyes I can walk in my gardens. I can touch in memory the cool petals of the flowers that will be blooming there, each to their season. I am almost able to smell the rich scent of the *Luculia* on a crisp winter day. I can lose the crowded, polluted city by imagining the intense sweetness of wallflowers, or the cool, damp earth after a shower of rain. I carry all these things with me, for as long as my personal timespan shall endure, and only then can there be an ending. In the present, after my travels I cannot wait to return to my work in the garen.

There is no conclusion, no finale, no denouement in gardeners' hearts, because our gardens fill us with a sense of continuity, of permanence. We know that this *Luculia* which rests its head against our windows today will be our companion again next season; that when flowers fade, the plant is merely resting, before returning to us again as the earth continues its universal cycle.

The garden engenders in us always a sense of anticipation, of looking with faith towards the future. In a few years, the saplings we plant today will bear fruit, become shade trees which will give pleasure to a future generation. These shrubs blooming today will be stronger, and their blooms more beautiful as the plant matures. Each successive season adds to the grace and beauty of our plantings.

This constant anticipation of joys to come precludes an epilogue for the garden, because there is always a going forward, a rebirth, regardless of whether it is aided or unaided by man. We may help and enhance it with our labour, but its continuity is self-perpetuated.

We have the gift of the changing tapestry which the change of the seasons paints upon the palette of the garden. We know that the very act of committing a bulb or seed to the ground with our own hands helps to perpetuate future life, but we also know that it is Nature herself who ordains its birth and growth, who engenders the miracle that goes on hidden from our sight beneath the soil.

The earth holds for us, with trembling secret, her treasures unborn. The garden, ever changing in its continual development of new life and eventual decay, reflects the changes which permeate our human lives. Because a garden is never finished, in this sense it is like the human world and all our undertakings.

This book, written to share with other gardeners, and whoever may care to read it, the pleasures, the pitfalls, the triumphs, the failures, the blood, sweat and tears of creating a garden from a wilderness where no garden existed before is also a tribute to these gardens which are now shared by many. Valley Homestead gardens have taught me much in the making, but a gardener's learning, like his garden, is never finished. In all our human endeavours we learn from the cradle to the grave, and never more so than in the cultivation of a garden. The gardener matures with his garden, each gardening year brings more learning, more knowledge gained, of plant names, their histories and habits, and of their cultivation.

The soil which is their cradle has been very much part of my horticultural learning curve too. Perhaps, one day, I shall even be learned enough to write the most erudite of tomes on the conversion of heartbreak clay to rich, dark loam which looks good enough to eat. The garden has taught me to look with seeing eyes, and to listen with hearing ears. It has fostered in me an awareness of shape, form, texture and colour, and is still teaching me how to create harmony and beauty in my combinations with these essentials.

So many worthy gardening oracles tell us, with the best of intentions, to do this and to do that, but they forget to tell us what we are doing it for. They are forgetful of the immense reward we receive in return for our labour. It is always 'Now is the time to do . . .', never 'Now is the time to look at, to stare, to listen, to touch, to pick, to feel, to enjoy, to be still, to laugh . . .'

They do not tell us to stop, put down our tools, to look from close quarters into the face of a flower; to close our eyes and breathe deeply of its scent. They do not tell us to commit the essence of such beauty to memory so that its ephemerality is immortalised. They do not tell us to hold in our palms' hollow or to close our finger around a dew-dampened rose or spray of blossom; to feel the fragility of the silk, the velvet of their petals.

They forget to tell us to breathe deeply of the fragrance of the soil or the scent of stock flowers after rain. They do not tell us to listen to the silence of our green seclusion, to the silent voice of colour, or to the breathing of the wind among the trees.

Spiritual feelings about one's garden are difficult to put into words. The gardens at Valley Homestead mean all these things to me. My gardening is the fulfilment of creativity, a source of immense and continuing pleasure. It is a gift of magnitude to be able to indulge a love of flowers, trees and of the natural world to the full, to be able to live at its green heart, work with it, share with it and love it.

We may get exasperated by the amount of labour the garden demands, but we continue our work, because this is our place of peace, of green, created with our own hands, where Nature herself is our guide and companion. She gives us the perception, through observation, to question on subjects such as why self-sown plants look stunning in places where we would never have dreamed of putting them, and why their germination has taken place with no help from us.

Dean Hole, writing in his book *Our Gardens* in 1889, tells of asking a lady how she would define the purpose of a garden.

He tells us that she replied, with rapturous disdain for the ignoramus who presumed to ask such a question,

What is a garden for? For the soul, sir, for the soul of a poet. For the brush of a painter! For visions of the invisible, for grasping the intangible, for hearing the inaudible, for exaltations above the miserable dullness of common life into the splendid regions of imagination and romance!

And there you have it.